Marmaduke Pickthall:

British Muslim

Marmaduke Pickthall: British Muslim

Peter Clark

Quartet Books
London   Melbourne   New York

Published by Quartet Books Limited 1986
A member of the Namara Group
27/29 Goodge Street, London W1P 1FD

Copyright © by Peter Clark 1986

British Library Cataloguing in Publication Data

Clark, Peter
    Marmaduke Pickthall: British Muslim
    1. Pickthall, Marmaduke—1875–1936
    2. Travellers—Near East—Biography
    I. Title
    915.6'042'0924   DS49

    ISBN 0-7043-2514-4

Typeset by MC Typeset, Chatham, Kent
Printed and bound by
Nene Litho and Woolnough Bookbinding
both of Wellingborough, Northants

To Anne,
who first told me of Marmaduke Pickthall,
and Felix,
for their Silver Wedding,
1961–86

CONTENTS

ACKNOWLEDGEMENTS

I have derived benefit from the magnificent services performed by the librarians of the Bibliothèque Nationale, Tunis, the Cambridge University Library, the London Library and the School of Oriental and African Studies in the University of London.

To many individuals I am indebted for ideas, encouragement, references and information. I would like to acknowledge debts to the following: Mr Michael Adams of the University of Exeter; Mr Hameeduddin Ahmed of Karachi; Mr Mir Sadat Ali of Hyderabad; Ms Martha Alleguen; Mr Mashouq Aly of the Islamic Foundation, Leicester; Ms Amanda Arrowsmith, County Archivist, Ipswich; Mr Muhammad Asad; Dr S.R. Ashton of the India Office Library; Mr Anand G. Chandavarkar of the International Monetary Fund, Washington and Hyberabad; Ms Isobel Clark of Pentlow; Mrs Anne Fremantle of New York; Mr Farid Gouverneur of the Islamic Texts Society, Cambridge; Mr William Hale of Hurstbourne Priors; Professor Muhammad Hamidullah of Paris; Ms Emma Hicks; Mrs Lina Hoffman of Damascus and Sana'a; Dr Derek Hopwood, St Antony's College, Oxford; Mr George Kassis of Aleppo and UNICEF; Mr M. Abdul Kareem Maher of Hyderabad; Dr R.C. Ostle of the School of Oriental and African Studies, London; Dr Robert Pacey of Toynton All Saints; Mr B.H. Qureshi of Karachi; Mr S. Sathyam of the Ministry of Education, New Delhi; Mr Abdullah Schleiffer of the American University, Cairo; Rev. D. O'N. Sealy of Tunis; Mr Mohammad Shafiuddin of Karachi; Mrs Mary Snell of Chillesford; Mr C.J. Sturman of Woodbridge School; Mr Rayner S. Unwin of George Allen and Unwin; and Mr Abdul Karim Winter.

To all my thanks. The shortcomings of this book are mine and mine alone.

My greatest obligations for enduring the invisible presence of Marmaduke Pickthall in the home for three years are to my immediate family: Theresa, Paul, Kate, Gabriel and Nathaniel.

PETER CLARK
La Marsa, Tunisia
1986

NOTE ON PICKTHALL'S PUBLICATIONS

Pickthall had the following twenty-five books in English published in his name. Further references are to be found in the bibliography.

1900 *All Fools*
1903 *Saïd the Fisherman*
1904 *Enid*
1905 *Brendle*
1906 *The House of Islam*
1907 *The Myopes*
1908 *The Children of the Nile*
1909 *The Valley of the Kings*
1911 *Pot au Feu*
1912 *Larkmeadow*
1913 *The Black Crusade*
1913 *Veiled Women*
1914 *With the Turk in Wartime*
1915 *Tales from Five Chimneys*
1916 *The House of War*
1917 *Knights of Araby*
1918 *Oriental Encounters*
1919 *War and Religion*
1919 *Friday Sermons*
1919 *Sir Limpidus*
1920 *Islam and Progress*
1921 *The Early Hours*
1922 *As Others See Us*
1927 *The Cultural Side of Islam*
1930 *The Meaning of the Glorious Koran*

He wrote extensively for several periodicals. I use the following abbreviations when reference in the notes or the bibliography is made to four of them.

IC Islamic Culture, Hyderabad
IR Islamic Review, Woking
IRMI Islamic Review and Modern India, Woking
NA New Age, London

INTRODUCTION

Marmaduke Pickthall is best remembered, when remembered at all, as a translator of the Qur'an, but he was also a novelist of whom E.M. Forster wrote in 1921 that he 'is the only contemporary English novelist who understands the Nearer East'.[1] Between 1903 and 1921 he published nine novels set in Syria, Palestine, Egypt, Yemen and Turkey. He also wrote six novels set in England, and short stories mainly about the Near East published in three collections.

In addition to his fiction, Pickthall devoted much of his time after his conversion to Islam in 1917 to writing and lecturing about that faith. For several months in 1919 he was Acting Imam of the Muslim community in London, preaching and publishing pamphlets. The last fifteen years of his life were based in India, and the lectures he delivered in Madras on 'The Cultural Side of Islam' were reprinted in New Delhi in 1981. His translation of the Qur'an, first printed in the United States in 1930, has since been reprinted several times in the United Kingdom, the United States, India, the United Arab Emirates and Libya.

The life and work of Marmaduke Pickthall were the subject of a biography written by Anne Fremantle in 1938, *Loyal Enemy*, and there is little to add in the way of biographical information since discovered. This book is not another 'life' but rather an examination of his writings and his ideas. Pickthall had no mentor, no disciples, and this accounts to some extent for his neglect. He was part of no movement, but rather an honest and perceptive observer, a lucid and vigorous communicator. At times he made colossal misjudgements, but his perception was not distorted by success, complacency or self-satisfaction. Because he was such an individualist his writings are not bound to the time of their composition, and seventy years later they may still assist in an understanding of the world of Islam.

1

Of that world he declared he was enamoured from his early manhood, and he penetrated it first of all by his conversion to Islam, then by living and working in India, not as part of the British imperial presence, but as an employee of Indians and finally as a pensioner of the Nizam of Hyderabad.

Part of the fascination of Pickthall's ideas lies in the fact that the sum of his views defies categorization. He was a monarchist and believed in the widest possible devolution of authority. He was critical of British imperialism in India, supported it in Egypt. He was a patriotic English Tory and opposed war between Britain and the Ottoman Empire, becoming thereby alienated from his fellow-countrymen. He was a man of openness and also a freemason. He combined gentleness in personal relations with ferocity in public controversy.

For twenty years of Pickthall's adult life he was a practising Christian. For the last twenty years he was a conscientious Muslim. An evangelical Christian would see his spiritual progress as that of a damned soul. A Muslim might see his embracing of Islam as his awakening to light. My aim is to describe the process with sympathy, refraining from any sectarian applause or censure. The first four chapters of this book are thematic and follow a rough chronological order. The first presents his background and Pickthall's career up to 1913. The following three take as central theme the three main issues that successively concerned him: Turkey, Islam and India. The principal source for these chapters is Pickthall's journalistic writings, documented in the bibliography, which amount to about half a million words.

The next two chapters examine his fiction. His short stories include some excellent pieces. His novels vary. He was more at home when writing on the Near East but there are some perceptive passages in his English fiction. He shows insight in dealing with the East Anglian poor of the late nineteenth century.

Six of his Near Eastern novels deserve to be re-issued: *Saïd the Fisherman, The Children of the Nile, The Valley of the Kings, Knights of Araby, Oriental Encounters* and *The Early Hours.* All, save *Knights of Araby,* are set in the Near East Pickthall knew. In the detail of personal habits, changing patterns of behaviour, turns of speech, social attitudes and physical description, these novels resemble photograph albums of the period. They disclose much that is inaccessible through the medium of scholarship. But as a novelist Pickthall is very much in a British tradition of novel writing. The best of the Near Eastern novels contain the circumstantiality of Sir Walter Scott, the exuberance of Charles Dickens, the moral strength of George Eliot, the compassionate tragedy of Thomas Hardy and the universality of E.M. Forster. I am suggesting not that Pickthall is as great as any of these but that his writings are recognizably influenced by the literary heritage to which these others have contributed. But what makes *Knights of Araby* and *The Early Hours*, two of his last novels, unique is that we have a mature and accomplished author writing the English Islamic novel.

Part I

1.

THE ARRIVAL OF A WRITER

'An Englishman of the English, an East Anglian.'
Larkmeadow

Marmaduke William Pickthall was born in Cambridge Terrace, London, on 7 April 1875, the son of Mary O'Brien (1836–1904) and the Reverend Charles Grayson Pickthall (1822–81).

On his paternal side Pickthall came from Cumbrian stock. Charles Grayson Pickthall was educated at Embleton, Buckinghamshire, and Christ's College, Cambridge. He was his father's curate at Broxbourne, Hertfordshire, for five years. There in 1856 he married Ellen Christie from a prosperous brewing family of Hoddesdon. In 1857 the living of Chillesford between Woodbridge and the Suffolk coast was purchased for him by the Christies and there Charles and Ellen brought up ten children before Ellen died in 1870. In April 1874 Charles married a widow, Mrs Mary Hale, at All Saints, Norfolk Square, London.

Mary Hale was the daughter of a colourful sailor, Donat Henchy O'Brien (1785–1857), who entered the navy in 1796. In the French wars he was captured off Normandy after a shipwreck, escaped from the fortress of Verdun and walked across northern France to the coast. Failing to get to a boat he was recaptured and conducted to the most notorious of French prisons of war, Bitche, near Sarreguemines. Here he eluded his captors and slipped across the Rhine bridge at Kehl, concealed and crouching among a noisy herd of cattle. After further adventures he was captured a third time and, under heavy chains, taken to Bitche. During his years in France he acquired great fluency in French and was able to pass himself off as a Norman to an Alsatian. His grandson inherited his talent for languages. O'Brien wrote a jaunty and readable account of his imprisonments and escapes in *My Adventures during the late War, comprising a Narrative of Shipwreck, Captivity, Escapes from French Prisons etc from 1804 to 1827.* These adventures were published in 1839 and an abridged edition was republished in 1902, edited by Charles Oman. Frederick Marryat plundered O'Brien's narrative for some of the incidents of his novel *Peter Simple.* O'Brien, after active service, reached the rank of Rear Admiral, married late in life and his youngest daughter was born when he was in his fifties.

Mary's first marriage was in 1859 to William Palmer Hale (1824–71), a barrister who published a few slim volumes of verse. The Hales had no children in the twelve years of their marriage.

Marmaduke was born just one year after his parents' marriage. A year later another son, Rudolph George – though known in the family as Bob – came on to the scene.

Pickthall's immediate family background was solidly professional middle class, assured and comfortable: the comfort of the brewery connection was however thinly spread with twelve children. Marmaduke spent the first few years of his life at the ten-bedroomed Rectory of Chillesford. His mother, from all accounts, was an independent minded lady. She had the reputation of not caring what she looked like and seems to have faced some resentment from her stepchildren. The Reverend Charles made a considerable impact on the tiny village, situated among the sand and woodlands of East Suffolk. In about 1860 he financed the restoration of the church, built a school and subsidized the salary of a schoolmistress. The west window of the church is in his memory and many of the church furnishings today date from the time of his incumbency.

Although Chillesford was Marmaduke's home for only the first five years of his life, he felt that his English roots were in Suffolk rather than anywhere else. He had a nostalgic view of a fading rural Arcadia: squire, parson and peasants supporting each other against cultural and economic invasion from the towns. He enjoyed and studied the dialect of Suffolk countryfolk. Three novels and many short stories were placed in East Suffolk.[1]

Marmaduke was not a robust young child. For health reasons he was circumcised and he survived a bout of bronchitis. In October 1881 his father died. The family was split up. His mother moved to 97 Warwick Gardens, London, and looked after the two small boys with the help of some of her stepchildren and an annuity of £900.

Marmaduke attended a day school in Kensington. He is reported to have had a retentive memory and was adept at mental arithmetic. But a brain fever at the age of eight set him back and also seems to have destroyed for ever his numeracy. He was then sent to Chillesford where his father's successor, the Reverend Beaufoy James Saint Patrick gave him lessons in the classics and inspired an interest in astronomy and wild flowers.

Mrs Pickthall moved house to Harrow on the Hill and Marmaduke entered Harrow School as a day boy in January 1889. In April his brother, Bob, joined him. Marmaduke was not happy at Harrow and left after six terms. He was good at geography and languages and enjoyed hymns in the chapel and cricket in the fields. He was in the Volunteeers and aspired to go to Woolwich and become a Royal Engineer. But like many a fifteen-year-old he was painfully shy and disliked the prevailing cult of idleness as well as the boisterousness and bad language of his contemporaries among whom were L.S. Amery and Winston S. Churchill. Pickthall's later recollections were of a life of vicious languor if we may judge from his last English novel, *Sir Limpidus*, which has a few chapters on Harrow school life.

He left Harrow at the end of 1890 while Bob stayed on. Mrs Pickthall took Marmaduke to Europe to improve his languages. He perfected his French at Neuchâtel and worked on his Italian in Florence. Mother and son returned to London and Marmaduke was placed at a crammer's in West London. What in the following century would be called a nervous breakdown was followed by coaching at Tonbridge and a realization that mathematical incompetence debarred him from becoming a Royal Engineer.

So in early 1892 Pickthall found himself as a boarder at St Catherine's School, Broxbourne, where the Reverend H. P. Waller coached him for examinations to enter the Levant Consular Service. In early 1894 he was a candidate for one of the two vacancies in the Service, but his interrupted and varied education took its toll. The examination included papers in arithmetic, Latin and English composition in addition to four modern languages.[2] Although he came first in the papers on languages, he was seventh on the list.

Pickthall was now thwarted in his attempts to enter two suitable professions and was at something of a dead end. A relation of his mother's first husband, however, had a friend, Thomas Dowling, who was about to go to Palestine as chaplain to Bishop G.F.P. Blythe, the fourth Anglican Bishop of Jerusalem. Mrs Pickthall gave Marmaduke the option either of rejoining his brother at Harrow and going on to Oxford or of going out to Palestine with Dowling. Pickthall later recalled that he considered himself 'an all-round failure, and was much depressed'. He accepted the more adventurous option, romantically setting his heart on 'Eastern sunshine, palm trees, camels, desert sand, as of a Paradise which I had lost by my shortcomings'.[3]

In raising funds for the trip his mother and family had the idea that if Pickthall learned eastern languages he might find some other way of getting into the Foreign Service. He set off for Marseilles, sailed to Naples and crossed the Mediterranean to Port Said. Soon earlier ambition, his own or what was wished upon him, 'lost whatever lustre it had had at home'.[4] He spent a few weeks in Cairo, wandered around the poorer parts of the city for which he felt great empathy and started to learn Arabic.

He went on to Jaffa and stayed in a Gasthaus in the German colony which he found dull until the Reverend J.E. Hanauer called on him. Hanauer was an English clergyman who had been born in Jerusalem. He was a major influence on the first part of Pickthall's adult life. He was fluent in Arabic and had been the interpreter for Sir Charles Warren when Warren, under the auspices of the Palestine Exploration Fund, was in charge of the first modern scientific excavation of the old city of Jerusalem, 1867–70. Hanauer loved Palestine and coached Pickthall in Arabic. He collected legends and folk tales and assisted Pickthall in appreciating the popular intellectual basis for otherwise unfamiliar beliefs and practices.

A second early acquaintance was an off duty dragoman, Suleyman, a wag and raconteur, who was staying at the Gasthaus. Suleyman, as Pickthall put it twenty years later, 'helped me to throw off the European and plunge into the native way of living. With him I rode about the plain of Sharon, sojourning among the fellâhîn, and sitting in the coffee-shops of Ramleh, Lydda, Gaza, meeting all sorts of people and acquiring the vernacular without an effort, in the manner of amusement.'[5] They travelled north to Carmel, east to Judea. They 'frequented Turkish baths; ate native meals and slept in native houses – following the customs of the people of the land in all respects. And I was amazed at the immense relief I found in such a life. In all my previous years I had not seen any happy people. These were happy people.'[6]

Suleyman introduced Pickthall to the Baldensperger family who had first come to Palestine from Baldenheim in Alsace in 1848 as missionaries. They had stayed on and pioneered beekeeping in Palestine. Pickthall travelled with various members of the family – to Ashkelon and Hebron. Like Hanauer, the Baldenspergers were scholars, interested in the language and beliefs of modern Palestinians. Pickthall was to review in the *Athenaeum*, in 1913, *The Immoveable East*, a collection of stories of Palestine by Philip Baldensperger.

After some months of such wanderings, when Pickthall 'turned up in Jerusalem and used my introductions, it was in semi-native garb and with a love for Arabs which, I was made to understand, was hardly decent.'[7] He spent the winter in Jerusalem, suffering the patronizing advice of longer established British expatriates. But in early 1895 Suleyman turned up and, with two hired horses and a muleteer, they went north to Tyre. Suleyman left to join his family. But Pickthall shortly afterwards met an Ottoman soldier, Rashid. Rashid persuaded Pickthall to buy him out of the army and allow him to be his servant.

With Rashid as a resourceful guide, Pickthall spent eighteen months wandering around Palestine, Lebanon and Syria. He stayed at 'Ain 'Anub above Beirut, a Druze village, the home of Dowling's predecessor, the Reverend W.H. Kelk. Kelk's Druze servant told Pickthall of the events of the civil war of 1860 when the Druze and Christians had fought each other in the Lebanese mountains and in Damascus. Pickthall wandered to Circassian Kuneitra, to Mount Hermon, to Moab and Transjordan, back to Palestine and Galilee and north again to 'Ain 'Anub. He travelled on among Druze villages to Homs and Hama. From 'Ain 'Anub – or from the railway station at 'Aley – he took the train to Damascus, 'the city of warm hearts and courtly manners',[8] as he later described it in a short story. In Damascus he was dissuaded from embracing Islam by the *Shaykh al-'ulama* of the Umayyad Mosque. As he recognized later, when he had become a Muslim, it 'was only the romance and pageant of the East which then attracted'.[9]

Pickthall lingered at 'Ain 'Anub and became friendly with the consul General in Beirut, Robert Drummond-Hay. Pickthall had the idea of purchasing a property and settling in the area and arranged to buy a house belonging to the Druze chief, Nasib Bey Jumblat. He concluded the deal with Nasib Bey and his Armenian creditor but Drummond-Hay intervened and forbad the transaction. Respect for past kindness from Drummond-Hay was mingled with frustration and the bitterness of incurring the supercilious scorn of other British expatriates.

As he recovered from the disappointment Pickthall fell ill with typhoid and was treated at the German hospital of the Knights of St John of Jerusalem in Beirut. He convalesced at Kelk's house in 'Ain 'Anub. Reports of his having gone native reached his mother who summoned him home. But before he left Lebanon he was offered the post of Vice Consul at Haifa, presumably by Drummond-Hay. The offer was withdrawn when his age – just twenty – was discovered.

He sailed to Smyrna (Izmir) and then travelled overland to Constantinople and through the Balkans, reaching England in early 1896.

The two years away determined the course of Pickthall's life. He left England a depressed boy, burdened with a sense of failure. He returned a man, not confident but buoyant and with a distinct identity. During those two years he mastered Arabic and was able to understand how the poor Syrian viewed the world. With Suleyman and Rashid as guides, he learned what the Syrians' amusements were, how they dressed, how they ate, how they slept, how they conducted business, how they thought. He observed, noted and contemplated. His Arabic tutor in Beirut, a Christian named Constantin, gave him *The Thousand and One Nights* as a leaving present in which, he said thirty years later, 'I see the daily life of Damascus, Jerusalem, Aleppo, Cairo and the other cities as I found them.'[10] He built a storehouse of memories that were to be the material for four novels and many short stories. He remembered flowers, smells, sounds, sunsets. The personality and psychology of the people he lived with, the people who were to swarm his novels, were set amid the blue skies, the olive groves, the red-roofed white-washed houses of Syria. It was the European with straw-coloured hair, red face, pith helmet and loud laugh who was out of place. And the Syrians who aspired to ape the Europeans were ridiculously alienating themselves from a gentler and more harmonious reality. Such were the attitudes Pickthall acquired during these two years.

In middle age Pickthall recognized that he had been bowled over by the romance of the East, by what he might reluctantly have acknowledged was a sentimental attitude. Yet the experience banished the depression. It provided him with emotional reserves. He saw in Syria a fraternity amid inequality, a joyousness amid hardship. There was – he perceived – no preoccupation with institutionalized material concerns such as wages or rent. His view was often naive but it was his love for, his interest in and his sympathy towards the ordinary unexciting unsung Syrian that was to be the source from which both the imaginative and the contemplative work of his life was to flow.

Pickthall arrived back in England shortly before his twenty-first birthday. He met an old sweetheart, Muriel, daughter of Cadwallader Smith. Smith was a former teacher and school inspector, in 1896 employed by a firm of educational publishers. Four years earlier, when Pickthall was at school in Broxbourne, he had proposed to Muriel and now, on his mother's urging, the two were married in London in September. Pickthall, conscious of marriage being a Christian sacrament, fasted before the morning marriage service.

It was a distant yet affectionate marriage. The partnership was childless and Pickthall developed austere views of marriage. He was suspicious of romantic love and, after he had embraced Islam – just halfway through the forty years of his married life – declared frequently that neither partner could or should rely on the other. 'The wife is a free servant of Allah, and so is the husband.'[11] But Muriel followed her husband to Turkey, to Lebanon and to India. He wrote regularly when they were apart and she followed him into Islam a few years after his conversion.[12] After his death she wrote a brief memoir of him for *Islamic Culture*. We have the impression of a loyal, uncomplaining wife, resignedly accepting a husband active in physical and intellectual wanderings. They never had a permanent home and, in England, occupied a series of rented houses in Suffolk, Sussex or in London.

The young couple went to Paris for a week's honeymoon. Their stay coincided with the visit of the Czar and Pickthall later recalled 'seeing in the Rue de Rivoli a banner bearing this inscription: "*Liberté, égalité, fraternité – et le Tzar.*" '[13] They went on to Geneva for the winter. Marmaduke was still suffering from the after-effects of the typhoid and was advised by doctors not to spend the winter in England. Pickthall was fond of Geneva, the lake and the mountain townships and placed several short stories in Switzerland. He was intrigued by the middle-class English people with their quarrels, their bad French and their elaborate social pecking order. He liked the Swiss villagers with their self-contained and introspective lives. Above all he loved the scenery of the mountains, watching the changing patterns of light on the water, learning to ski and writing.

The years after Syria were a bit of an anticlimax. Pickthall tried to settle down to a life of writing and his first publication was a Swiss tale, 'Monsieur le President', which appeared above the ridiculous nom de plume of E. Greck in *Temple Bar* in January 1898. Until the end of 1899 the Pickthalls had no fixed base. Marmaduke was in London during the winter of 1897–98 and spent many hours wandering around the streets of the capital. The following winter he was in Switzerland again, staying at Geneva and at Champéry. He met Mrs Skene, widow of a British Consul who had been in Aleppo in 1860 when Lebanon was in turmoil and when riots tore Damascus apart.

But Pickthall was mainly concerned with writing and getting things published. His first Near Eastern story, 'The Word of an Englishman', was published in *Temple Bar* in July 1898. It is an intense tale of an unfriendly village on the Syrian coast. There was much of it that anticipated the best of his Near Eastern writings: an eye for detail and colour, for the perspective of Syrians and an appreciation of the excellent reasons why a Syrian village should be hostile to outsiders. This tale appeared the following month in *Littell's*

Living Age, a weekly literary magazine, published in Boston, Massachussetts.

In 1899 the Pickthalls could not even afford a servant and were living on a diet of 'bread, cheese and milk.'[14] Genteelity was restored in November 1899 when they took a house, at £65 a year, in the village of Holton, one mile from Halesworth in north-east Suffolk. Ash Cottage was small but with extensive grounds, 'an excellent garden, winding pinewoods, a paddock, a coachyard, small group of farm-buildings, tennis-court, more pinewoods, and a fine stretch of heath on which is a picturesque windmill. There are eight acres in all.'[15] Ash Cottage was Pickthall's home for five years. The village is thinly disguised as Larkmeadow in the novel of that name. Pickthall took an active part in village life. He was chairman of the Parish Council, an enthusiastic supporter of local activities and produced a village performance of *The Mikado.*

During the last years of the century Pickthall was simultaneously writing two books – both based on his own experiences. The first was what he initially called 'The Bunny Book' and became *All Fools,* a farce of life based on a Kensington crammer's establishment. The other was far more serious and thoughtful and became *Saïd the Fisherman.*

At Holton also he wrote two Suffolk novels: *Enid* and *Brendle.*

His first novel, *All Fools,* was rejected by two publishers, John Lane and Fisher Unwin, before Swan Sonnenschein accepted it. It was published in March 1900 and sold at six shillings. There was a print run of six thousand. After the success of his second novel, *Saïd,* Pickthall bought up and destroyed remaining copies of *All Fools,* disowning it. It is not mentioned in works of reference for which he supplied the details.

Two years later Pickthall had difficulty in finding a publisher for *Saïd the Fisherman.* It was rejected by Fisher Unwin and also by an American publisher. An agent managed to place the book with Methuen at the end of 1902 and it was published, again price six shillings, in July 1903. At the beginning of August there was a most enthusiastic review by A.J. Dawson in the *Athenaeum,* comparing Pickthall to James Morier, the author of *Hajji Baba of Isfahan.* 'It is in more respects than one a remarkable book; it belongs to a little exploited school of fiction, and is one of the very best of its select school that we have came across.'[16] James Barrie and H.G. Wells joined in praise of the book. *Saïd* was published later in the year in the United States, and one American journal announced that as far as England was concerned, Marmaduke Pickthall had 'arrived'.[17]

For the next few years he was to publish a novel each year. His first Suffolk novel, *Enid,* was published by Constable in June 1904. In spite of praise from the *Athenaeum*, it did not repeat the success of *Saïd*. At the end of the year Pickthall disposed of Ash Cottage and moved to Fordingbridge in Hampshire. He appears to have suffered from depression: frustration, perhaps, at his inability to sustain the momentum of *Saïd*. Also at this time his mother was dying of cancer.

His second Suffolk novel, *Brendle*, was published in September 1905 by Methuen. After its publication he moved to London and took a flat in Maida Vale for all of the year 1906. A second Near Eastern novel, *The House of Islam*, a sad disappointment after *Saïd*, was published in September 1906. Pickthall seemed set to be a one-novel man. During 1906 he received a letter from a stranger, Lady Valda Machell. Lady Valda was born Victoria Alice Leopoldine Ada Gleichen and was a daughter of Prince Victor of Hohenlohe Langenburg. Her husband, Percy, had been a British army officer in the Gordon Relief Expedition, joined the Egyptian army in 1886 and, after twenty years Egyptian service, was, in 1906, adviser to the Minister of the Interior in Cairo. The Machells were on leave and Lady Valda invited Pickthall to tea at St James's Palace. A warm friendship was born, followed by an invitation to come and stay with the Machells in Cairo.

Pickthall had not been back to the Near East for ten years. In 1904 plans for a visit had been abandoned because of his mother's illness but in early 1907 Pickthall crossed from Marseilles to Alexandria; and the next few months in Egypt and Syria gave a new impetus to his creativity.

Pickthall arrived in Cairo as the guest of a British official. During 1907 he met other imperial servants and publicists. Some such as Aubrey Herbert and George Hornblower became friends. He became a dissenting acquaintance of others such as George Lloyd, Mark Sykes and Valentine Chirol. Percy Machell was a cousin of Thomas Russell (Russell Pasha) then in the early years of a forty-year police career in Egypt.

One would expect Pickthall from his sympathies with the people of Syria and from his later career, to have been a critic of British rule over eastern people. On the contrary, he was and remained a great admirer of Cromer and his work. In 1907 Cromer was at the end of what Pickthall called his 'autocratic, but benevolent and upright reign'[18] of twenty years as British Consul General. Pickthall called on Cromer and suggested that the Ottoman Empire be more closely associated with British rule. This, in Pickthall's view, would please the Egyptian people and reduce the powers of the Khedive. Cromer replied – according to Pickthall after Cromer's death – :'I fancy it will come to that.'[19]

Pickthall combined a respect for Cromer's firm rule with a disdain for the slogans of the Nationalists. In later years he saw Cromer and himself as witnesses of an Islam that had passed away: 'the then existing structure in Islamic countries, including despotism and a host of abuses and anomalies, but including some heroic qualities which made it dignified and certain true Islamic qualities which made it lovable.'[20] Cromer, he wrote in 1914, 'was a soldier to begin with; but he possessed a grasp of affairs which the cleverest of politicians might well envy, besides a bent for honest, solid work. He never made the least pretence at understanding the Egyptians or consulting them; but did what he himself and his advisors considered needful for the good of Egypt.' For Pickthall had no sympathy with modern western ideas of constitutionalism. Compassionate, subtle and benevolent despotism within a prescribed moral and political system was preferable. Kitchener was too heavy-handed as Consul General in the years before 1914. His appointment was like 'moving heavy artillery against butterflies.'[21]

When Pickthall arrived in early 1907, Egypt was still full of talk of the 'Denshawai incident'. In June 1906 some British army officers had been pigeon shooting near the village of Denshawai near Tanta in the Delta. There were misunderstandings about whether they hand the permission of the village authorities. The villagers whose livelihood depended largely on pigeons, when they saw their threshing-ground burning, blamed the officers and attacked them. Guns were fired, two villagers were killed, one officer collapsed and died. The official verdict was that he died of sunstroke and concussion. Villagers were rounded up and a special tribunal imposed heavy sentences: four were sentenced to hang, two to penal servitude for life. Others were imprisoned and lashed. The hangings and lashings were carried out in the village of Denshawai in the presence of the villagers.

Liberal opinion in Egypt and Britain was shocked. But Pickthall did not share in the outrage. He accepted the severity of exemplary punishment. Pigeon-breeders, he argued, were not the mild folk that you might expect. Pigeons caused damage to crops and pigeon breeders were 'the most turbulent among Egyptian villagers'. He reckoned that the advent of a Liberal government in Britain – in December 1905 – had led to expectations of nationalist unrest. 'It was known in Egypt that English Liberal Governments demand Nationalist movements; so a Nationalist movement was at once inaugurated.' The British rule was beneficial. 'The Army of Occupation stands for English rule in Egypt; and English rule in Egypt stood at that time for things which did not exist in neighbouring lands – things like religious toleration, personal security and some attempts at even-handed justice.' It was not too much to say that a British uniform at that time stood 'for the personal security of every Christian in Egypt. If that uniform had been violently insulted with comparative impunity ... the consequences would have been infinitely more horrible than was the punishment of Denshawai.'[22]

Pickthall had an independence of mind that was almost unpredictable. He was often unsentimental and pragmatic. But his stance on Egypt in 1907 coincided with that of the more imperially minded British officials of Cairo. It was not the romance or obligations of Empire that determined his attitude but rather an informed sympathy with the lot of ordinary Egyptians. During his months in Egypt he wandered extensively in the Delta and in upper Egypt and collected tales, impressions and observations that were the staple of two novels and many of his more perceptive short stories. He was aware of the great gulf separating Englishmen and Egyptians. Englishmen were symbols of authority and justice. These symbols had to be upheld for what they represented. On the other hand the symbols led to expectations, the disappointment of which led to frustration that found solace in the slogans of the Nationalists. Two of Pickthall's Egyptian tales show how Nationalists are created through this process.

While he was in Cairo Pickthall received a letter from J.E. Hanauer, now chaplain at Damascus, inviting him to stay. He accepted the invitation and in Damascus the two men worked through a great collection of legends and folk tales that the chaplain had collected. Pickthall took them with him back to Europe. He met Muriel in Marseilles and together they wandered in Corsica and Italy before reaching England where Pickthall prepared Hanauer's collections for publication.

J. E. Hanauer's *Folklore of the Holy Land* was published by Duckworth at the end of 1907. Pickthall wrote an introduction in which he showed his interest in the syncretism of the main religions of Palestine and the sharing of traditions between Christians and Muslims. Jesus and his mother were revered by Muslims, just as Christians had reverence for the Caliph 'Umar. Although, Pickthall wrote, after the Islamic conquest the Christians 'were deprived of their church-bells they kept their churches; and if large numbers of them embraced El Islâm, it was through self-interest (or conviction) and not at the point of the sword as has been represented.'[23] Pickthall also wrote some footnotes based on legends that he had come across. *Folklore of the Holy Land* has several tales that were used by Pickthall in *Oriental Encounters*.

Pickthall did not have a steady relationship with any one publisher. His first three novels were brought out by three different publishers. Methuen, who published *Saïd*, also brought out *Brendle* in 1905 and *The House of Islam* in 1906. In November 1907 *The Myopes* was published by John Murray who also published his next three novels. Then between 1912 and 1917 six books appeared, one a year, each published yet again by a different publishing house. Only after 1917 did he stick with William Collins, although it was Allen and Unwin who in Britain published *The Meaning of the Glorious Koran*. *The Myopes* was poorly reviewed but ten months later *The Children of the Nile* appeared and was better received. The Egyptian visit had revived anew his imaginative creativity.

In September 1908 he returned to Egypt, this time taking Muriel, and stayed with George Hornblower for six weeks. Cromer had now retired and Pickthall was not impressed by the hesitations of his ailing successor, Sir Eldon Gorst. While in Cairo he heard the news of the annexation by Austria of the Ottoman provinces of Bosnia and Herzegovina. This was a few months after the Young Turks' revolution and Pickthall shared the Ottoman sense of betrayal. The revolution turned the Ottoman Empire towards European examples. Why then was Austria permitted by the rest of Europe to get away with the annexation of part of the Empire in violation of the 1878 Treaty of Berlin?

In December the Pickthalls went on to Lebanon, staying first with English friends in Beirut, then at a hotel before moving to the mountains and taking a house where they lived for five months. This was Muriel's longest spell in the Near East. Marmaduke passed time with the village schoolmaster studying Arabic, observing his fellow creatures, listening to conversations and scribbling, collecting material for more short stories. He took Muriel to Jerusalem several times and she met the dragoman, Suleyman, who was now blind. But life in Lebanon exhausted their financial reserves and the couple returned to England after a trip to Damascus to see Hanauer.

In May 1909 the Pickthalls rented a large house in Buxted, Sussex, called Five Chimneys, which became their home for six years. Both Pickthalls were enthusiastic country dancers and Muriel taught dancing to the villagers. They kept up a large garden and Pickthall wrote his short Palestine novel, *The Valley of the Kings*, published by Murray in November 1909.

His first collection of short stories, *Pot au Feu*, was brought out by John Murray in February 1911. His last Suffolk novel, *Larkmeadow*, based on his Holton years, came out in August 1912 and *Veiled Women*, on the harims of Egypt, in January 1913. As well as his fiction, from 1909 he was writing articles on Near Eastern themes for several journals. He earned enough from his writings to have holidays away from Sussex. In the winter of 1911 he was at St Cergues, ski-ing with the Machells. In other years he undertook some mild mountaineering in Switzerland, he cycled in France and made less strenuous trips to Belgium, Holland and Italy. It was a conventional life.

But, as his journalism indicates, he was getting more and more involved with eastern politics. He felt angry that revolutionary Turkey was assailed by hostile evangelical propaganda; that European powers were taking advantage of her. Buxted had a good railway service to London and Pickthall was frequently travelling to London, making common cause with like-minded publicists in defence of the Ottoman Empire.

Pickthall contributed articles principally to the *Athenaeum* and the *New Age*. His reviews for the *Athenaeum* were usually on contemporary novels or on books about Turkey, Palestine and Egypt. He reviewed a lot of unmemorable novels with titles like *Did Cupid Count?* and the *Broken Halo*. In his reviews of books on the Near East he was often pedantic about the use of travellers' Arabic. He used the opportunity to puff Hanauer's work on the folklore of Palestine. He looked at novels with Near Eastern themes but thought often that the author had 'not probed into the minds of the inhabitants'[24] – in unspoken contrast to his own novels. In 1913 he reviewed a new edition of *Eothen* by A.W. Kinglake, first published in 1844, observing from it 'the tremendous changes which have taken place in the administration and social life of Turkey since the work was written; while the life of Egypt, underneath the tourist and official surface, remains much the same.'[25]

From 1912 he began an association with the *New Age* which lasted until Pickthall left England for India in 1920. The *New Age* was a weekly, edited by A.R.Orage, a journalist of skill and guile. He used to persuade successful and established writers like Arnold Bennett and John Galsworthy to write for it for nothing. George Bernard Shaw did not write but helped to keep the journal financially afloat. Meanwhile Orage published the early work of young writers whose reputations were made much later – G.D.H.Cole, C.E.M. Joad, T.E. Hulme, A.S. Neill, Ezra Pound, Richard Aldington, Ruth Pitter and Katherine Mansfield. Politically the line of the *New Age* was radical, even socialist – Orage was at this time a Fabian in the process of being disillusioned – but it was a forum for independent and dissenting approaches to affairs of the world. Pickthall wrote on 'eastern subjects' and repeated his pro-Turkish themes right through the First World War: which is an eloquent testimony to the relaxed nature, in this context, of British censorship.

Pickthall's first articles in the *New Age* were on Egypt but in 1912 when the Balkan countries were at war with Turkey, releasing sentiment for Bulgaria and hostility towards the Ottoman Empire and Islam, Pickthall began to pour out his inmost feelings, feelings that led him in the next few years to declare himself a Muslim.

In November 1912 he wrote a series of articles under the title, 'The Black Crusade', which the New Age Press later published as a pamphlet. In these articles Pickthall displayed his ferocity of feeling in expounding Turkey's rights and wrongs. He deplored the assumed sympathy of European Christians for Bulgarians, Serbs and Greeks. There may have been legitimate Balkan Christian claims, he acknowledged, but 'when one hears (as I did lately) in an English church, the Turks compared to Satan, the Bulgarian advance to that of Christian souls assailing Paradise, one can only gasp'. It was 'as if Muslim blood may be shed more lightly (they would not put it so, but it amounts to that).'[26]

At the same time he wrote a more temperate article for the prestigious *The Nineteenth Century and After*. In this he argued that there was a tradition of toleration in the Ottoman Empire. 'Of old, poor Christians and poor Muslims lived on equal terms, chaffing each other freely on the subject of religion, as many genial folk-tales live to witness.'[27] It had been foreign interference – missionaries and consuls – in the nineteenth century (and after) that had led to privileges and advantages awarded to the indigenous Christians, resented by their Muslim compatriots. Pickthall pointed out that the Turks in 1908 'alone of all Mohammedans have stepped out of the Middle Ages into modern life'.[28] His article prompted a reply in the same journal by Sir Edwin Pears who had been a resident of Constantinople before Pickthall was born.

It had been Pears who in 1876 had raised the alarm about Bulgarian atrocities, stirring political and emotional feelings that lingered on for half a century. 'A plague upon the blessed word "Bulgaria".' was Pickthall's reaction. 'It was brought out automatically, as the cuckoo from the clock, "our fellow-Christians", "horrible atrocities", "sacred name of Gladstone" and "unspeakable Turk" – a whole array of pseudo-pious catchwords as inappropriate to the present conflict as "Abdul the Damned".'[29]

The Revolution in Turkey had brought Muslim progressives to power, men who looked for inspiration to and support from England. Pickthall had been brought up as a Tory. 'Among the things I was brought up to admire,' he recalled just before his death, 'was Disraeli's Oriental policy by which England was to become the mentor of the Islamic world, to foster and assist its revival, using Turkey as interpreter and intermediary.'[30] A mutual sympathy between the Young Turks and Britain was a natural consequence, especially as the Treaty of Berlin, signed by Disraeli, was supposed to uphold Turkish territorial integrity. Turkey was made to honour her obligations under the Treaty but the European Powers made no effective protest when Bosnia and Herzegovina were annexed by Austria, Bulgaria declared her independence, Italy invaded the province of Tripoli and the Balkan Christian states invaded European Turkey.

Turkish reform, Pickthall argued, was a threat to the Christians of the Ottoman Empire. 'They hated the idea of Moslem progress.'[31] The implications of the attacks on Turkey were global. 'The Moslems of the World have seen sheer acts of brigandage encouraged by the Powers against a Moslem state, and this dastardly and cruel war acclaimed as a Crusade by Christian Europe.'[32]

Such were Pickthall's views at the end of 1912 when he decided to go to Turkey to see for himself.

2.

A HEART IS BROKEN
PICKTHALL AND TURKEY

'A fine race is being hounded to its death by Europe
because it is too proud to plead, and cannot beg.'
Pickthall in 1914[1]

Turkey in 1913 had lived under a constitution for five years. The
Young Turk Revolution of 1908 was a political revolution that was the
culmination of a century of developments in the Ottoman Empire.
The autocracy of the Sultanate had been steadily eroded for two or
three generations. In order to be effective, this autocracy needed
innovations and the gadgetry of nineteenth-century industrialism.
These innovations required technicians and an educated class that
looked to western Europe for their textbooks, training and ideas of
efficiency. In July 1908 a secret organization, the Committee of Union
and Progress, which had widespread support in the army, compelled
the Sultan Abdul Hamid to restore a constitution with a parliament
and responsible government and to abolish censorship. Men who
had spent years in exile returned as honoured citizens. For several
years after 1908 power remained in the hands of men, often elderly,
who were cosmopolitan in their outlook, French in their education,
liberal in their views, aristocratic in their background and elitist in
their instincts.

In the years after the 1908 Revolution Turkey faced war with or
threats of war from most of her neighbours and in 1912 an alliance of
Balkan states invaded European Turkey with voracious territorial
demands. The last months of 1912 and the first part of 1913 were

critical for the Turks. Salonika fell on 8 November. In December Edirne, the Turks' first capital in Europe, a city of national and religious as well as strategic importance, was under siege. On 23 January the most charismatic of the Young Turks, Enver, an army officer, carried out a *coup*. He entered the session of the Cabinet and forced the aged Anglophile Grand Vizier, Kamil Pasha, to resign. The Minister of War, Nazim Pasha, was shot. A senior soldier, Mahmud Shevket Pasha, became Grand Vizier. His Cabinet was dominated by members of the Committee of Union and Progress, known as Unionists. A tougher line with the pursuit of the war was expected. In Istanbul the new Unionist Minister of the Interior, Jamal Pasha, imposed a curfew and tighter censorship.

Pickthall had rejoiced in the Turkish revolution and wanted to see the beleaguered capital for himself. The publisher, Eveleigh Nash, gave him an advance on the royalties for *Veiled Women*, published in January 1913, and Pickthall travelled to Istanbul via Berlin and Constanza and thence across the Black Sea to Galata. He arrived in March with letters of introduction from Aubrey Herbert and pursued his own contacts. For two weeks he stayed at the Pera Palace Hotel in present-day Beyoğlu, but had an aversion to the importunate sleeziness of Frenchified Pera. 'Contrasted with the stricter morals and puritanical decorum of the Turks, Pera and its neighbour, Galata, are a huge plague-spot – a parasitic growth which threatens Turkey with corruption.'[2]

Through a Turkish friend he was able to arrange to take rooms at the village of Erenköy, on the Anatolian side of the Bosphorus. Erenköy was a prosperous dormitory village and its inhabitants people of substance. He stayed at the house of a German lady, Fraülein Kate Eckerlein, who had lived for many years in Turkey. Her name was modified by the Turks to Misket (Miss Kate) Hanum. Pickthall found the Erenköy atmosphere quite different from that of Pera. 'Real Eastern cries were wafted from the distant roadway. I felt entirely comfortable and in place for the first time since leaving my own Sussex farmhouse.'[3]

Pickthall filled in time learning Turkish. He studied first with a Roman Catholic Arab from Diyarbekr, a teacher at the Galataserai school. His second teacher was *Imam* at the mosque of Göztepe, a progressive who was all for modernity without in any way compromising his own Islamic beliefs. Pickthall practised his Turkish though at first he spoke with an Arabic accent. By the time he left he was able to discuss politics and to read newspapers.

His two best Turkish contacts were both closely involved with public affairs. The first was Ali Haidar Bey, son of Midhat Pasha, the reforming Grand Vizier of the 1870s, who had fallen foul of Sultan

Abdul Hamid. The other was the Foreign Minister, Prince Said Halim, a grandson of Muhammad 'Ali, Viceroy of Egypt. Pickthall described in a letter to Muriel his first impressions of Prince Said Halim. He had 'very blue eyes, very brown cheeks, very white collar, very black frock-coat, very red fez which looks like a part of his head, and a cigarette in an amber holder stuck permanently in one cheek. Very neat, correct and automatic in his movements – just like a toy'[4]

He often crossed from Erenköy to Istanbul by train and ferry. 'There was always a coterie of persons from my village who always gathered in the same coach of the train, the same position on the steamer. I soon became a recognized familiar of this group, which comprised ex-Ministers of State and high officials; officers employed at the arsenal or the Ministry of War, doctors, khôjas, and some journalists.'[5] On his arrival at Galata bridge, 'like everyone else who comes to town from country places where the roads are deep in dust or mud, according to the season, I had my boots cleaned'.[6] He would wear a fez and if the sun was strong would take a parasol. He would lunch at a restaurant and have his favourite dish, stuffed vine leaves. He called on his Turkish friends or on *The Times* correspondent, Philip Graves.

There is no evidence that he looked up his antagonist, Sir Edwin Pears, who, at seventy-eight years of age, was still living in Istanbul. Pickthall was critical, even contemptuous, of British residents in Turkey who were often tied to European business interests and

> were unfairly sceptical of Moslem progress. Their attitude of irritation and impatience is easy to explain. Unconcerned with the views or aspirations of their Mohammedan neighbours, their aim is to secure the comforts and to lead as far as possible the life of Western Europe. Thus they find themselves in conflict with the Oriental spirit, and demand its abolition or subjection for their own convenience.

Their natural allies were the Levantines of Pera and they adopted 'in time the Pera point of view, forgetful of its radical injustice. For Pera is unblushingly, fanatically parasitical; its population preys upon the empire with intent to kill; and the same may be said with truth of the Christian quarter of almost every seaport town in the Levant.'[7]

Pickthall, in contrast to most European visitors, pursued and cultivated only Muslim Turks. His perception of Turkey was more intimate than his perception of Syria or Egypt. As a youth he was introduced to Syria and Palestine through missionaries. He repudiated these contacts and developed his own, but the contacts were limited. In Egypt he came to the country as the guest of British officials. These he did not repudiate. But in Turkey his first contacts were well-informed Liberal Turks. As on his earlier travels he identified with the people of the country through language and dress.

The Turkish Liberals saw reform as a process to be carried out by educated and cultured gentlemen familiar with European ways – men like themselves. They had opposed the autocracy of Sultan Abdul Hamid because he had refused to share power with them. The rule of law and a rational system of government would be established when they were in power.[8] The Unionists were more abrasive, usually of a lower social class, and attained influence by way of the increasingly meritocratic army. Unionists often spoke only Turkish. Erenköy was a Liberal village and most of Pickthall's friends were Liberals, 'but two or three – and those the best I had – were Unionists.'[9] Misket Hanum herself was an ardent supporter of the Unionists.

High party feeling was intensified on 23 June 1913 when the head of the Unionist-dominated government, Mahmud Shevket Pasha, was assassinated. Some Istanbul observers saw the assassination as revenge for the murder of Nazim Pasha in January. The tough Minister of the Interior, Jamal Pasha, rounded up murderers and conspirators while others lay low or slipped out of the country.

Pickthall revered Mahmud Shevket Pasha and saw him in almost Messianic terms. He was 'the most hard-working and sincere of patriots,'[10] 'the one man whom I knew to have the will and capacity to save his country from the hundred enemies inside and out, who threatened its existence, and to save El Islam from undeserved humiliation.'[11] The assassination caused public consternation – 'Quiet men, who had till then disowned both parties, were now Unionists.'[12] Pickthall sympathized with the government's stern punitive measures. 'Twelve were hanged. To show you the value of a punishment which seemed to me excessive: a very peaceful, law-abiding Syrian merchant whom I knew, being in Stamboul, went to see the bodies hanging on the gibbets, and touched one of them. He told the tale with placid satisfaction. "Then I felt more comfortable," he said, "for then I knew for certain that we had a government."'[13]

Pickthall came to Turkey expecting to like Turks – he was not disappointed. By contrast he was never fair to Ottoman Christians, who always appeared to him as arrogant, insinuating and self deluding. They did not know when they were well off, was Pickthall's attitude. The Ottoman system guaranteed autonomy and a measure of freedom. There had been no Smithfield in Turkey. (Sir Edwin had disagreed with Pickthall on this.) Allegations of Muslim fanaticism were belied by the facts, not only of social relations but also of official practice. At one particularly intense period of the Balkan wars,

> a prelate of the Greek Church in Constantinople died, and was buried there with full ceremonial, Turkish troops keeping the road for the procession. Suppose a Roman Catholic army to threaten the city of Belfast – the parallel was suggested to me by an Englishman who had just come from the North of Ireland – and a Roman Catholic bishop to die just then, would he be allowed a public funeral?[14]

Writing to Muriel, Pickthall poked gentle sarcastic fun at the Christians. 'There was a glorious row in the Greek Church at Pera on Good Friday; four different factions fighting which was to carry the big Cross, and the Bishop hitting out right and left upon their craniums with his crozier; many people wounded, women in fits. The Turkish mounted police had to come in force to stop further bloodshed.'[15]

It was the Muslim Turks who displayed tolerance, a greater tolerance than their European partisans. Misket Hanum on one occasion received some Turkish officers on leave from the front. Pickthall noted his surprise 'to find that her vituperation of the Bulgars was neither echoed nor applauded by these actual fighters.'[16] Reformed Turkey was embittered when, having accepted toleration as an official ideal, she was subject to further hostilities. Pickthall's enthusiasm for the Turks increased the longer he stayed in the country. He was critical of Turkish indifference to the Arab provinces and was scornful of the idea of a parliament for Syria ('A parliament! A water-melon!', he expostulated.)[17] He noted that Turks could be punctilious, pedantic and humourless, yet he saw Turkey as the hope of the Islamic world.

The Revolution of 1908 promised an age of reform. From this Pickthall anticipated an improved and educated Islam. Fanaticism was no part of Islam, and education, he averred hopefully, eradicated fanaticism. It gave Pickthall much satisfaction to meet men of religion who were avowed progressives. Exhortations to tolerance in the Qur'an outnumbered advocacy of intolerance. Moreover the Turks were adherents of the Hanafi school of Islam, 'the only Sunnite sect of El Islam which accepts man's reason as a guide before tradition'.[18] As such she had a role to play. 'Turkey is the present head of a progressive movement extending throughout Asia and North Africa. She is also the one hope of the Islamic world.'[19] Turks should recognize their Islamic heritage rather than attempt to pose as

Europeans. Arabic and not French should be their second language.

Muriel went out to Turkey in June, shortly after the assassination of Mahmud Shevket Pasha and stayed a few weeks before returning together with Pickthall by boat in July. Marmaduke described their final departure.

> Slowly, almost imperceptibly, the quay receded. The crowd piled upon it became a mist, the volleys of farewells no longer audible; only the flutter of the handkerchiefs could be distinguished. That also vanished, and the city claimed our eyes. The tugs cast off; the steamer throbbed to life. The glorious vista of the Golden Horn, the old palace and the lighthouse, the Mosque of Sultan Ahmed slipped away, to be restored to us far out at sea in one vast panorama with the hills of Asia. We sat on deck and watched it till the sun sank.[20]

Pickthall went out to Turkey as an observer. His stay only strengthened his partisanship for the reforming Muslim Turks. He saw, as the progressive imams saw, that there was no conflict between modernization and Islam. In later years Prince Said Halim elaborated a conservative philosophy of modern political Islam. Pickthall broadly agreed with these views and expounded them fourteen years later in his lectures on Islam delivered in Madras.

The most significant personal impact on Pickthall of these four months in Turkey was that, with prejudices reinforced, he became politicized as never before. Always intense and sincere, he returned to England with passionately held convictions of the merits of Turkey's leaders, the need for the British government to give them support and – if the word is not inappropriate – to crusade against misrepresentations of Turkey and the Turks.

On his return, Pickthall had an article published in the September number of *The Nineteenth Century and After* on the Islamic reformers of Turkey. Between September 1913 and January 1914 his account of his time in Turkey was serialized in the *New Age*. The series was significantly entitled ' A Pilgrimage to Turkey during War Time'. In March 1914 the articles were published in book form by J.M. Dent as *With the Turk in Wartime*.

Henceforth he became more and more active in meetings and committees. As war approached Pickthall wrote regularly in the *New Age* of the Russian threats to Turkey. His activities were not restricted to journalism. He became involved with a group of politicians and publicists who sought to secure an unfashionable hearing for Turkey. The supporters of the Anglo-Ottoman Society, founded in January 1914, of which Pickthall was an active official, included a former British Ambassador to Constantinople, Sir Louis Mallet; the independent minded Conservative member of parliament for Taunton, Aubrey Herbert, who had travelled extensively throughout the Ottoman Empire; Professor E.G. Browne of Cambridge; the romantic Scottish aristocratic socialist R.B. Cunninghame Graham; and the more straightforward Labour leader, James Keir Hardie. Before the war broke out Pickthall made two attempts to secure employment in Turkey. Both failed.

Britain went to war with Germany in August 1914. Pickthall argued strongly for Turkish neutrality and independence. He was not a pacifist and was ready to be a combatant so long as he did not have to fight Turks. Events in the autumn swept on inexorably and on 5 November Britain declared war on Germany's ally, Turkey. Pickthall declared himself 'heartbroken at the turn events have taken'.[21]

These events did not budge Pickthall from his loyalties. Throughout the war he wrote article after article in the *New Age* advocating consideration for Turkey's case. He maintained a quixotic and principled consistency while the world went mad. There were four consistent themes in Pickthall's articles. First, he claimed to adhere to an old English foreign policy. Secondly, he warned against what he saw as the pernicious influence of Russian policy. Thirdly, he repudiated the idea that Balkan Christians could claim special protection from Britain by virtue of their being Christians. And fourthly, he pressed the positive merits of the Turks, the glorious revolution of 1908 and the coming and consequent regeneration of the Islamic world.

In the three months between the declaration of war with Germany and of war with Turkey Pickthall wrote a series of articles, 'Turkish Independence'. In these he argued that

> from the days of Queen Elizabeth there was a growth of English policy towards firm alliance with the Porte, an independent, friendly Turkey being regarded as the strongest bulwark of the British Empire in the East. Disraeli – a great genius – working on that ancient policy, evolved the finest plan for the good use of the Empire that any nation ever threw aside.[22]

Disraeli, he argued, loved both England and the East and

> wished England to become the benefactress of the East, its guide to freer life and more enlightened institutions. He had the wit to see that this great work could be achieved only by the intermediary of a strong and independent Eastern State. No better for his purpose

could be found than the Ottoman Empire with its headship of the Muslim world.[23]

Under the influence of Gladstone, Britain repudiated this policy, to the distress of Turks themselves. When this Anglo-Islamic policy foundered, when 'England threw Disraeli's scheme with the old policy aside, it was at once picked up by Germany'.[24] Turks 'only turned to Germany . . . after England failed them'.[25]

This displacement by Germany of Britain had come about as a result of the machinations of Russia, which had become the 'chief Power in the Triple Entente'.[26] Russia was behind the project of the Balkan States' assault on Turkey. Russian interests threatened the territorial integrity of Turkey and, in the long term, the British Empire in India. Pickthall saw a conspiracy of silence about atrocities perpetrated by the people of the Balkans against Turks and Muslims. *The Times*, he suggested, was being censored by the Foreign Office. Articles on Turkey had 'a tone of hostile menace thinly veiled by the pretence of giving good advice to forward children.'[27]

Russia had exploited a factitious feeling of Christian brotherhood. Because the Balkan nationalities were (largely) Christian, it was argued, we should have more sympathy for them than for Muslims. The British press were interested only in offences and outrages committed by Turks and Muslims. Pickthall recalled that he was in Germany in February 1912. The newspapers were full of the reports of atrocities committed by Christians. Such reports 'were at that time ridiculed in England' whereas in Germany 'pamphlets on the subject had the place of honour.'[28]

In contrast to this Pickthall hammers away at the qualities of the Young Turks. Shortly before the war he wrote in the *Athenaeum* that the 'Turks are hard to know. They do not talk about themselves, and rather snub the curiosity of Western journalists.'[29] At the end of 1914 he started another series of articles called 'Six Years', tracing the transformation that the Ottoman Empire had seen since 1908 and stressing the promise these changes had for the whole of the Islamic world. The rule of the Sultan Abdul Hamid, portrayed with such venom by European observers, was equally unpopular with Turks.

> The discontent was not apparent; it could hardly be so; and many Europeans resident in Turkey . . . divided by a bridgeless gulf from Turkish life, were ignorant of its existence . . . . . The Turkish revolution, therefore, took all Europe by surprise. Yet the current of it had been swelling unobserved for years. The current was Mohammedan and National, having nothing in common with the movement of the Paris group of Turks.[30]

Within a few years all sorts of reforms had been carried out. There was an expansion in education, brigandage was suppressed, a new pride arose in being Turkish. Pickthall recalls saintly Mahmud Shevket, who

> had an exquisite home life and hankered for it always, regarding all his public efforts as mere toilsome interludes. He honestly believed that there were other men, by hundreds, far better fitted than himself to fill high offices of state. And so he was for ever hanging back from opportunities which most men would have pounced on. His was the true spirit of the Committee of Union and Progress which regarded personal ambition as a poor delusion.[31]

When news of ill-treatment and massacres of Armenians reached England from the autumn of 1915 onwards Pickthall squarely faced the challenge to his loyalties. In November 1915 he wrote an article in which he does not dispute the facts of massacres but attributes the blame to all but the Turkish government.

> Let us try to understand what has actually happened. Some Armenians, in Armenia proper, Turkish subjects, rose in arms and betrayed the town of Van to the Russians. When the news of this occurrence spread throughout the Empire, the common people in some places rioted against Armenians, just as the people in the East End of London rioted against the Germans upon the news of the sinking of the *Lusitania*, but with this difference, that the Arab and the Kurdish mobs, being three hundred years, at least, behind the London mob in civilization, did what the London rabble of three centuries ago would have done, and killed their victims. Following on these disorders the Turkish Government ordered the removal of the whole Armenian population from the war zones to concentration camps of some sort – as much with a view to their protection, it seems but fair to suggest, as with a view to prevent further treachery. When the Turkish forces retook Van, there was a slaughter of Armenians in that district by the Kurds, their ancient enemies, who . . . were armed with Russian rifles before the war, at a moment when the Turks were wishing to disarm them . . . But it is all one to the enemies of Islam – and they are powerful just now in England – since Kurds are Muslims of a sort . . . They are enemies to Turkish government in times of peace, and very uncongenial and distrusted friends in time of war. And it must be remembered that the Armenians, in their native land, are far from being the sheep-like, inoffensive crowd that they are sometimes painted. They also, when at war, commit atrocities.[32]

A Heart is Broken: Pickthall and Turkey

The young Arnold J. Toynbee wrote a pamphlet that autumn on Armenian atrocities. Pickthall reviewed it in the *New Age* on 25 November 1915. Again he does not deny the fact of atrocities but diverts attention from the specific to the general and to the implications of Toynbee's line of argument. Toynbee writes of the disgrace of some Armenian girls. 'These were Christian women, as civilized and refined as the women of Western Europe and they were sold into degradation.' In return Pickthall asks:

> What does Toynbee mean by that? Does he mean that the peasant girls and women of Armenia are as civilized and refined as English ladies of the wealthy classes, or as the girls and women of a Suffolk village, or as the harridans of a London slum, or as the prostitutes of London and Paris? The statement is unnecessary, and it seems to me deplorable, because it is an appeal to the religious fanaticism, being based on the fanatical and altogether false assumption that Christians are intrinsically better than Mohammedans, and their lives of more worth. That assumption, inculcated by the foreigner, whether as a private missionary or as the intriguing agent of a foreign Government, is at the root of all the troubles in Eastern Anatolia, where a Christian minority has been taught to regard itself as of infinitely more importance than a Mohammedan majority, and has been egged on to sedition, anarchism, and rebellion with the notion that Christians ought to rule over Mohammedans, being intrinsically superior.[33]

In official circles during the war Pickthall came to be regarded as a security risk. His talents as a linguist and as an authority on Syria, Palestine and Egypt could have been used but his reputation as 'a rabid Turcophile' prevented him from being offered a job with the Arab Bureau in Cairo, a job that went instead to T.E. Lawrence.[34]

In 1916 Pickthall attempted, in a most unorthodox way, to make private diplomatic initiatives. Dr Felix Valyi, who edited *La Revue Politique Internationale* from neutral Switzerland, was in touch with the Turkish government. Pickthall wished to go to Switzerland to build bridges between the British and Turkish governments. Not surprisingly, his application for a passport was refused. Pickthall was quite open in his activities, sending copies of letters to Sir Mark Sykes, MP, then an adviser to the government on Near Eastern policy. Sykes wrote pompously to Pickthall: 'I do not consider that it is proper that you should assume absolute friendship to an enemy state . . . and further speak in a distinctly hostile tone of your own Government.'[35] Valyi should correspond with the British Military Attaché in Berne, proposed Sykes.

This snub inhibited Pickthall's international activities but did not prevent his continuing to campaign for a separate peace with the Turks. He spoke at public gatherings and became active in 1917 and 1918 in the politics of Muslims in London. In July 1917 he addressed a meeting at Caxton Hall. Pickthall's proposal of a separate peace mission with the Turkish government alarmed one listener, a Persian Armenian, Malcolm (or Melkom) Khan, who conferred with the Zionist leader, Dr Chaim Weizmann. Both feared the consequences to Armenian and Zionist aspirations of the neutrality of Turkey and protested to the Assistant Secretary of the War Cabinet, William Ormsby-Gore. Any intention there may have been of involving Pickthall or Aubrey Herbert on a peace mission was abandoned.[36]

In the last months of the war Pickthall was called up and became a private in the 17th Hampshires and was stationed at Southwold on the east coast of Suffolk. He found the rough comradeship of the ranks an agreeable way of life after the tensions and frustrations of middle-class agitation when he was at issue with most of his countrymen. He had recently declared himself a Muslim. But, 'pitchforked, so to speak, at forty-three, among all sorts of men', he found 'a Muslim point of view a very godsend, making me content where I should once have been extremely miserable.'[37] At the end of the year – at the end of the war – he was promoted to the rank of corporal in charge of an influenza isolation hospital. He became a civilian again in March 1919.

The public effect of Pickthall's wartime activities was total failure. There is no evidence that he influenced anybody or in any way affected the course of events. It is not difficult to find fault with some of his journalistic writings. He sometimes wrote, as he acknowledged, 'at fever-heat and without the proper journalistic reference to Blue Books and the *Encyclopaedia Britannica*'.[38] He was writing often week after week for a magazine with a fixed copy date. He could be as tiresomely arrogant as the British expatriates whom he met in Palestine when he was an eager young man. Like them he claimed a special authority as a result of his own particular experience. Like them, this led him to project ethnic stereotypes. 'I may claim to know a little about Eastern character, and I know that the Oriental loves a keen, enthusiastic worker in authority, even though ill-tempered, brutal, or a martinet. The languid type, which lets things take their course or does its duty merely, he does not admire; he sees too much of it.'[39] His defence of the Turkish government of 1914 was based on his personal knowledge of the members of that government. He was prepared to base arguments on hearsay but if the same methods were used by others in the lively correspondence columns of the *New Age*, he would be exacting in his demands for supporting evidence. When, on one occasion, he was cornered into acknowledging that Turkey had breached the terms of her neutrality before she was at war with Britain, he feebly admitted that there 'have been faults on both sides'.[40]

His polemical journalism quickly became out of date, not least when he made predictions that were to be totally wrong. If Britain were to depose the Egyptian Khedive, he predicted shortly before the British deposed the Khedive, 'it would cause much horror and rebellious feeling' and 'he and his descendants would become the hope of El Islam at once'.[41] After the deposition rebellious feeling was contained and the deposed Khedive rapidly sank into ineffectual obscurity. Nothing could be more unpopular, Pickthall foresaw, than the suggestion that Turks 'should discard the fez and take to hats'.[42] The change in headgear, if not popular, met with little resistance. After the change Pickthall argued that the matter was 'unimportant'.[43] His loyalty to the Committee of Union and Progress outlived the committee. In 1919 the Committee was eclipsed for ever. Yet Pickthall thought the Committee, 'though at present in eclipse, is not extinct. It is greater now than in its day of power, because more popular. The Young Turk Ministers, in their misfortunes, have a following of half the world. The East, which we have scorned, is with them; and the whole East seems to me upon the point of rising – against us.'[44] He became an admirer of Atatürk but took care to note in 1932 that Turkey's revival was due not to Mustafa Kemal alone but also to the Committee of Union and Progress.[45]

A more serious moral charge against Pickthall is that of racial prejudice. In the intensity of his indignation he could not bring himself to recognize any merits in the Balkan Christian states. Austria's reaction against Serbia in June 1914 after the assassination of the Archduke Franz Ferdinand was quite legitimate. 'Austria declared war upon the nose-cutting Serbs, and Germany prepared to back her in the undertaking, in exactly the same spirit with which we should send a punitive expedition against Thugs or cannibals, supposing they had killed an English prince.'[46] His prejudice becomes something uglier when he wrote of Armenians as a 'race of traitors, spies, blacklegs, perjurers, lickspittles, liars, utterly devoid of shame or honour. That is the Armenian nation in the eyes of Asia at the moment. To kill them is as good a deed as to kill scorpions. They defile the globe. It is not a pleasant thing to write, but it is true.'[47]

Pickthall saw himself as a spokesman for Asia. Passions roused by warfare during and immediately after the First World War produced many similar words of racial hatred. They do not exonerate Pickthall. It is possible to argue that Pickthall was consistently pursuing the logic of his loyalty to the Turkish wartime government. It is possible to present Pickthall as showing courage in facing the issue and articulating a Turkish point of view. But such excuses do not lessen the utter insensitivity Pickthall displayed towards Armenians at a time of unprecedented human suffering. The only qualifications to these expressions of brutality is that his more considered writings, his novels and his religious writings, show far more charity, enlightenment and dignity.

Flawed though Pickthall's wartime journalism was, his writings have historical interest. He drew attention to aspects of the Ottoman Empire that were not at the time appreciated at all in Britain. His short-term specific expectations were woefully fallible, but he was sounder in longer-term assessments. He argued strongly for maintaining the integrity of the Ottoman Empire. He anticipated a fragmentation of authority in the culturally diverse areas of Syria, Mesopotamia and Kurdistan. What, he asked in 1915, is going to replace the Turkish empire 'when those provinces are suddenly erected into independent States? Syria would be in tribal war for fifty years, Beyrout would be sacked and burned a score of times before, in the course of nature, she evolved a sovereign State, and then, I think, she would evolve not one, but several.'[48]

There are two themes that emerge in these writings which, seventy years later, stand up to the passage of time. The first is the significance of the Young Turk Revolution of 1908, how it was an attempt to salvage a remarkable political institution – the Ottoman Empire – and how that revolution was Islamic. The Ottoman Empire had its own dynamism, its own procedures, its own political systems for dealing with ethnic, religious and cultural minorities. Other westerners who welcomed the 1908 revolution, welcomed the Europeanizing features of modern Turkey. Turks, they seemed to suppose, became civilized as they became more like Frenchmen or Englishmen. The Ottoman Empire, in its extent and durability, was the most successful Islamic empire in history. Islam was the basis of the Turkish empire and Pickthall saw, as few other westerners saw, that the Young Turks were inspired by a reforming Islam that demanded education, social improvement and enhancement of the status of women. All this was in accordance with the Prophet's example and teaching.

The second theme was the universality of Islam. The war years were years of emotional turbulence for Pickthall. In 1917 he declared his conversion to Islam. The cause of Turkey was only one aspect of Islamic politics. The Prophet had deplored nationalism. Islam and not nationality was the pointer to identity. Until 1914 Pickthall's own direct experience of Muslims had been Syrian Arabs, Egyptians and

Turks. But during the war he became aware that the cause of Turkey was the object of Muslim concern everywhere. He got to know Muslims from India. The collapse of the Turkish empire threatened the Caliphate, the *khilafa*, the political importance of which was upheld by Muslims far beyond the confines of the Sultan-Caliph's political jurisdiction. The cause of the *khilafa* was to take Pickthall to India.

During and immediately after the war, periods of personal stress and turmoil, Pickthall wrote two novels that are among the best things he ever wrote. One, *Knights of Araby*, was published in April 1917. The other, *The Early Hours*, published in 1921, tells the story of a Turkish soldier between 1908 and 1913. It covers the ground of his polemical journalism but avoids its embarrassing faults. It is as if Pickthall found solace in eluding the world of harsh reality and creating his own world of fiction. Politics and the deadlines of journalism fostered stereotypes. Those stereotypes vanished when he was able himself to give flesh and personality to Turks and Armenians and to place them in the olive groves of Thrace or the offices of revolutionary Istanbul.

3.

THE TURN OF THE TIDE
PICKTHALL AND ISLAM

1. By the morning hours
2. And by the night when it is stillest,
3. Thy Lord hath not forsaken thee nor doth He hate thee,
4. And verily the latter portion will be better for thee than the former,
5. And verily thy Lord will give unto thee so that thou wilt be content.

The Glorious Koran (Sura XCIII)

Pickthall's background was one where adherence to the Church of England was the rule, indeed the obligation. Both his father and his father's father were clergymen. Two of his step-sisters were Anglican nuns in South Africa. Another, Grace, used to make regular visits to Chillesford, where the father had been Rector, until her death in 1962.

It was through church contacts that Pickthall first went east. But he was unimpressed by the European Christian community in Palestine, whom he found too frequently snobbish and sectarian. The young Pickthall was an oddity to the established comfortable middle-class missionaries when he chatted in fluent colloquial Arabic with the servants. Near Eastern missionaries were to provide the main material for *The Valley of the Kings* (1909) and *The House of War* (1916). By the time of the First World War he saw the missionaries as misguided menaces who, with spiritual arrogance and political ineptitude, were alienating the Christian subjects of the Ottoman Empire and undermining that Empire itself. 'The whole thing seems to me, and always seemed to me, intolerably vulgar.'[1] At the end of the war he recalled that even

> in the days when I supposed myself to be a Christian it used to seem to me disgraceful that a country so enlightened as my country claims to be should allow and, even as it seemed in some instances, encourage Christian missionaries to annoy non-Christians by their attempts to proselytize within the boundaries of the British Empire, an Empire which I had been taught to regard the home or rather school of civil and religious liberty.[2]

During his two years in Palestine and Syria he was tempted to embrace Islam. He was dissuaded by the *Shaykh al-'ulama* of the Umayyad mosque in Damascus. 'Wait till you are older,' the old man advised, 'and have seen again your native land. You are alone among us, so are our boys alone among the Christians. God knows how I should feel if any Christian teacher dealt with a son of mine otherwise than as I now deal with you.'[3]

In the years of his early manhood in England and Switzerland Pickthall resumed the role that conformed with his Anglican background. He was married in a church and was a regular communicant. He was a Highchurchman, upholding the Apostolic succession and the obligation of fasting. A friend and Oriel contemporary of his brother, T.W. Hickes, was ordained a deacon. Pickthall in some ways envied Hickes' calling, in particular 'the qualities which make your vocation a true one. A clergyman's life is, I consider, or may easily be, the most artistic of which our modern life admits.'[4]

In the fictional writings produced during his twenties and thirties he portrays a range of clergymen. They can be absent-minded but benevolent as in *The Myopes*, or snobbish and malevolent as in *Brendle*. There are no crises of conscience. Religious obligations and spiritual introspection are absent.

In the years immediately before the war Pickthall continued to be a practising Anglican. He was on excellent terms with his vicar at Buxted. During his visit to Turkey in 1913 he worshipped at the Crimean Memorial Church in Istanbul. But the exploitation of Christian sentiment for the sake of sympathy for the Christian subjects of the Sultan disgusted him. And when in 1914 a Church of

England congregation, in his presence, sang the hymn of Charles Wesley with the call to

save
The souls by that imposter led:
The Arab thief, as Satan bold
Who quite destroyed thine Asian fold,

Pickthall could no longer participate. He 'slipped quietly from the church and from Christianity.'[5] But not at once openly into Islam.

Pickthall's loyalties to two empires, the British and the Turkish, were stretched to breaking point when war broke out between them. He suffered a nervous and spiritual crisis. The first years of the war were occupied in efforts to explain the Ottoman government. The first of the two novels published at the time, *The House of War*, reflected in fictional form the points he was making in his regular articles for the *New Age*. The second was *Knights of Araby*, a serener novel of the middle ages, without any European characters. In contrast to his journalism, there is a placidity and good humour in *Knights of Araby*, a book in which all the characters are Muslims.

By 1917 there are small shifts in the content of his journalism. References to Islamic beliefs have increased and the Qur'an is quoted more frequently. In January 1917 he wrote for the first time for the *Islamic Review and Modern India*. His first article for this main organ of British Islam was a prose hymn of praise for the Prophet as an historical character, 'the minutest details of whose conduct and demeanour are recorded for us by his own contemporaries'.[6] 'To the last he was a pious Muslim, simple in his habits, regular in prayer, vigorous and far-seeing in affairs of state, gentle and forgiving in his private intercourse with men, a loyal friend, a *noble* enemy, faithful in all things that he undertook.'[7]

In the summer and autumn he gave a series of talks to the Muslim Literary Society in Notting Hill, West London, on 'Islam and Progress'. During the last talk of the series, on 29 November 1917, he declared openly and publicly his acceptance of Islam. The lecture hall was crowded. He argued that Islam alone was a progressive religion. Other religions were unfit to claim that their tenets countenanced progress. He quoted frequently from the Qur'an in Arabic. His intonation, in the words of one who was present,

threw those who were not used to listening to such recitations from a Western's lips into ecstasies. From start to finish Mr Pickthall held his audience as if in a spell by his erudition, by his deep thinking, and lastly by the most genuine and rocklike faith with which every word of his breathed into the splendour and beneficence of Islam. The way in which he concluded this most impressive utterance was still more moving. With his hands folded on his breast, and an expression of serene contentment on his face, he recited that famous prayer which concludes the second chapter of the Holy Qur'an. When he sat down, every one of his hearers felt that they had lived through, during that one short hour, the most remarkable period in his or her life.[8]

Pickthall took on the name Muhammad and immediately became one of the pillars of the British Islamic community.

Before 1914 the chief centres of organized British Islam were Liverpool, London and Woking.[9]

In 1887 a Liverpool solicitor of Manx origin, W.H. Quilliam, embraced Islam after visiting Morocco. In 1889 he was the leader of a small community and from 1891 rented a house in Broughton Terrace, West Derby, for prayer meetings. His first converts were his own family, including his mother, Harriet. He published a number of pamphlets – such as the *Faith of Islam* and *Fanatics and Fanaticism*. From 1893 to 1908 he issued a weekly, the *Crescent*. He claimed up to 150 British adherents to Islam and undertook social work in the interests of spreading the faith. Medina House was a home for foundlings who were cared for and brought up as Muslims. Quilliam built up international Islamic contacts. He became the Persian Consul in Liverpool and received 'a personal gift' from the Amir of Afghanistan. With this money he purchased the West Derby premises which were used as an Islamic Institute and a residence for himself and his family. Quilliam travelled around Britain and lectured on Islam, using non-Islamic networks like Manx Clubs and Temperance Societies. He lost some public credit in 1896 when he issued a proclamation to Egyptian soldiers, about to embark on the reconquest of the Sudan, urging them to refrain from taking up arms against their Muslim brethren. Quilliam left England in 1908 and his son, Bilal, sold off the West Derby premises. The Liverpool movement seems to have petered out after that.

In the generation before 1914, London's transient community of Muslims, mainly students from India, was growing. An Islamic Society existed from 1907. This was the successor to the Pan-Islamic Society which itself had taken over from Anjuman-i-Islam, founded in 1886. In the years before 1914, prayers were held at private houses or in hired halls – at Lindsey Hall, Notting Hill Gate, and at Caxton Hall. Larger rallies were occasionally held in Leicester Square, at Hyde Park Corner or on Peckham Rye. The Society issued a monthly journal, *Light of the World*, and reprinted Dr Stubbs' *Rise and Progress of Mohammadanism.* In 1904 Khalid Sheldrake claimed to be 'the only Englishman' among worshippers who included Indians, Egyptians and subjects of the Ottoman Empire.[10]

In the 1880s a ruler of the Indian state of Bhopal was persuaded by a Hungarian orientalist called Leitner, registrar at the University of the Punjab, to leave funds for the construction of a mosque in England. The mosque was built at Woking, Surrey, in 1889 and was named after the ruler, Shah Jehan. A student hostel was attached. By 1913 the mosque and adjacent buildings were in a neglected state.

In that year three events gave a boost to the British Muslim community.

The previous year a Lahore barrister left a successful practice in his home town and came to England with the objective of disabusing the Western mind of wrong notions about Islam and of working for conversions. Khwaja Kamal-ud-Din was to become the leading personality of the British Muslim movement for the following twenty years. Kamal-ud-Din was born in 1870 into a family of scholars and poets and was educated at the Formal Christian College, Lahore. He was a professor and then Principal of the Islamia College, Lahore, before he took up law. On his arrival in England he based himself at Richmond, Surrey, and held meetings at Hyde Park Corner before moving to Woking in the summer of 1913 to start the Woking Muslim Mission. Khwaja Kamal-ud-Din was a powerful personality with much energy and a command of trenchant English. He was of a large build and physically dominated the small group of worshippers whom he led in prayer. Some Muslims in Britain have seen him as a controversial figure. He was involved in the Ahmadiya movement and some even deny that Kamal-ud-Din was a Muslim. It cannot be gainsaid however that he was adept at making friends and gave a coherence previously lacking to British Islam. On the analogy of the Chief Rabbi, the British press referred to him as the Very Reverend Khwaja Kamal-ud-Din. Pickthall, who did not always see eye to eye with him, called him the 'ambassador of Islam'.[11] Under Kamal-ud-Din Woking became a social centre of British Islam, an essential port of call for foreign Muslim dignitaries. Visiting Indian princes, in later times the Amir Faisal of Saudi Arabia and the Amir Abdullah of Transjordan, all made their way to the mosque at Woking. Khwaja Kamal-ud-Din suffered from ill health and went to India for prolonged medical treatment. He would be away from Woking for months at a time – once for over a year – visiting outlying corners of the British Empire and making contact with Muslims.

In the autumn of 1913 Kamal-ud-Din produced the first number of the monthly *Muslim India and the Islamic Review.* In the following years it changed its name to *Islamic Review and Modern India* before settling down to the *Islamic Review* in 1921. Its earlier titles indicate the major source of inspiration for Islam in Britain. Under the editorship of Kamal-ud-Din it had the qualities of weighty Victorian quarterly and parish magazine. The *Islamic Review* gave regular news of conversions with reports from the press on Islam. It kept its readers informed of activities, religious and social. Articles explained points of the faith and of Islamic law. Half a page in each number had a statement of faith, in transliterated Arabic, which readers were invited to declare, sign and despatch to Woking. One enthusiast regularly wrote an article on Islam in Esperanto. From the early numbers of the review one gains an insight into the community's activities. The portraits and group photographs of well-dressed and middle-class men and women at fashionable London tea-rooms could have been of Quakers or rationalists. Like Fabians but unlike Masons women were prominent and active in the movement. Analogies cease when we note the international interests and the large number of Indians and Egyptians in the activities of British Islam.

The third event of 1913 significant for Islam in Britain occurred in December when a member of the House of Lords, the eleventh Baron Headley, announced that he was a Muslim. Headley was not the first peer to do so. Lord Stanley of Alderley, an uncle of Bertrand Russell, had become a Muslim half a century earlier. Headley was a civil engineer and had worked in India. He threw himself into the activities of the British Muslim movement. He wrote frequently in the *Islamic Review* and performed the pilgrimage with Kamal-ud-Din in 1923. Headley's conversion drew the attention of the curious British public to Islam, not as the wild religion of half-civilized mullahs and mahdis, but as a faith that might be personally relevant to British individuals.

These three events galvanized Islam in Britain and gave it a measure of acceptability. A core of British converts, mostly middle class, kept in touch with each other and worshipped together on the occasion of the major festivals in the Islamic year. Many had worked overseas, in Islamic countries and especially in India, and had been impressed by the faith and conduct of Muslim colleagues. Around this core was a larger population of transient visitors to Britain, often students from Islamic countries, notably India but also from the Malayan peninsula and West Africa. In 1924 it was reckoned that thirty regularly attended prayers at the Woking mosque, that there were a thousand British Muslims scattered about the country and 10,000 Muslims from overseas. Among the British Muslims was a polymath Professor Henri Marcel Leon who wrote in a range of languages, including Turkish, on many subjects – sleep, reptiles and the Manx language. Other active Muslims included Ameen Neville J. Whyment Ph.D., Professor Noor-ed-Din Stephen, Yahya John Parkinson and Major and Mrs R. Legge and their children Ahmad, Safia, Saleem and Jameel.

Pickthall's declaration of his faith in November 1917 was the turning point of his life. Round his declared faith he picked up the pieces of his emotional and personal life that had been shattered by the war. He identified himself totally with the world Islamic community and at the end of 1920 went off to India.

A new serenity enters his life. There is, in his writings, less striving for effect. He no longer uses obscure words. With a personal tranquillity there is also an urgency in what he writes. In December 1919 he published *Sir Limpidus*, the last of his English novels. In March 1921, his Turkish novel, *The Early Hours*, appeared. His last collection of short stories came out in October 1922, when he was in India. After that he published two short stories. Everything else he wrote and published was related in some way to Islam; and though Islam changed direction for him, there is no variation in the quality of what he wrote. *Sir Limpidus* is readable but otherwise no worse than his other English novels. *The Early Hours* is as good as the best of his eastern novels.

After the act of declaration before witnesses Pickthall advanced at once to a position of leadership among British Muslims. Within a few months he was leading prayers at the mosque in London. In April 1918 he gave a sermon on 'The Kingdom of God'. In early 1919 he was officiating at the Friday prayers in London. The *Islamic Review* reported that his

> sermons have been characterized as much by his great scholarship and erudition as by his skilful and masterly elucidation of the popular Qur'anic themes. His recitations of the Arabic texts have been most inspiring. Our English friends will, we trust, have rejoiced to see one of their own race lead in prayers in Arabic a congregation of mixed races.[12]

During much of 1919 Khwaja Kamal-ud-Din was out of Britain on extended sick leave. Until an assistant arrived in the autumn, Pickthall, in recognition of his knowledge of Arabic, was Acting Imam of the London mosque, the Muslim Prayer House in Camden Hill Road, Notting Hill. The sermons preached were published at Woking as *Friday Sermons*. He led the prayers at Woking for *'Id al Fitr*, the feast that concluded the fasting month of Ramadan, in June 1919. For several months he was Acting Editor of the *Islamic Review*. At the same time he pursued his Islamic political concerns and in October

1919 chaired a Day of Prayer for the Khalifa at the Muslim Prayer House. In his address he attacked the Western powers for presuming to decide who should be Khalifa. 'The question of the Khilafat is no concern of Christians any more than it is the concern of Muslims to decide who shall be Pope of Rome . . . The Muslim world as a whole accepts the Ottoman Sultan as its Khalifah with enthusiasm and impassioned sympathy.'[13]

In the course of his sermons and addresses he recited verses of the Qur'an in Arabic. He also rendered them into English. This piecemeal translation became the fragments from which he constructed his last major work. He felt a special responsibility as a leader of British Muslims. They were, he said, 'in a position of the early Muslims in Mecca, in the days when they were looked upon as weak and neglible'. They had a duty to dispel false notions. 'Make your Islam respected and believed in your own circles, and give the lie to those who say false things about the Faith.'[14]

Pickthall boldly undertook pastoral responsibilities of advising and even chiding his flock. In 1920 he was critical of the behaviour of foreign Muslim students in England. He conceded that:

There are excuses for them. The change from a state of society in which grown women hide their faces and the outline of their forms in public is subversive. The temptations which assail newcomers from the East at every turn are inconceivable by Europeans. But the harm done to Islam by the misconduct of a Muslim here in England in inestimable. It gives English people an utterly false idea of Islamic notions of morality. Muslims are extraordinarily strict in regard to the relations of the sexes; they condemn all looseness of behaviour with regard to women. Who would think it, I ask you, seeing the behaviour of some Muslims here?[15]

He was understanding about the difficulties faced by 'the little band of Muslims of pure English birth' during Ramadan. A Muslim is obliged to fast during the lunar month from sunrise to sunset. In 1918, 1919 and 1920 the fasting month fell during the summer when a Muslim in England would be required to fast for up to eighteen hours. We cannot alter that, said Pickthall. The difficulties remain and it

behoves us, therefore, to observe the fast of Ramadam to the utmost of our power . . . If you accustom yourself to occasional abstinence from permitted things, the necessary things of life, you learn to see them as the blessings that they really are, and grow content with them; you lose your craving for things harmful and unnecessary.[16]

He was practical in his advice to those who had never fasted before. They should 'take just enough to keep yourselves from feeling faint – a cup of tea, say, with a slice of bread, when you get up, again at about two or three o'clock. If you do that during the whole of the month you will find that next year you can keep the fast completely.'[17]

Pickthall wrote prolifically on different aspects of Islam in the nineteen years between his public embracing of Islam and his death. He identified himself with the world Islamic community and talked of 'we Muslims'. He was punctilious in the performance of his religious obligations, praying regularly and showing a total disregard for personal possessions and even for his own personal privacy. He fasted in Ramadan but did not find the obligation easy. Muslims are required not to smoke during the daylight hours of Ramadan and Pickthall was an addictive smoker and puffed at cigarettes or a pipe as he wrote. 'I can do without food and drink,' he wrote, reflecting the feelings of many other Muslims, 'but not without smoking.'[18] He never performed the pilgrimage. Well advanced plans for doing so went astray.

Muslims who knew him recall him as being 'a good Muslim'. Just as there was an honesty and an accuracy in his fictional writings, so there was an integrity and a sincerity in his religious life. He was a witness to his faith. He preached, wrote, explained and encouraged. He undertook the mighty task of rendering the Qur'an into a form that made it accessible to Anglophone Muslims.

Between 1917 and 1920 most of his writings on Islam appeared in the *Islamic Review and Muslim India*. Some were series of articles and sermons and were reprinted as booklets. In addition to *Friday Sermons*, a short series of addresses in 1919 on war were printed as *War and Religion* at Woking in 1919, translated into Indonesian and published at Bandung. Addresses he delivered in 1917 were published as *Islam and Progress* at Lahore in 1920. He wrote frequently and at speed. The distillation of his Islamic thought appeared in a series of lectures he delivered at Madras in 1925. They were reprinted in *Islamic Culture* and published in 1927 as the *Cultural Side of Islam*. The book has had a happy publishing history. It was republished by Ferozsons of Lahore in 1958 under the title *Islamic Culture*, and by Kitab Bhavan, New Delhi, in 1981 with its original title and is still in print.

For one half of his adult life Pickthall was a practising Christian, for the latter half a practising Muslim. It is possible to see from his writings how he saw a common kernel of belief in the two religions. The declaration of faith for a Muslim is the *shahada*, the declaration 'There is no God but God, and Muhammad is the Prophet of God.'

The first part was an unexceptional article of faith for a Christian. 'If you examine carefully,' Pickthall preached in 1919, 'the various great religions of the world, you will find that they all set forth one truth originally, and preserve some vestige of it still behind the mass of superstition. That truth is the Eternal Unity of God.'[19] An acceptance of the overwhelming power of God was common to Pickthall's faith as a Christian and as a Muslim. It was the duty of all to exalt, honour and submit themselves to God. 'If we serve our friends, or our relations, or our country, or our religious community without that personal adherence to Allah which is the duty of every one of us, without the thought of Allah's universal purpose, we exalt our relations, or our country, at the expense of other men's relations, other people's countries, and we are really doing them harm instead of good, in terms of humanity.'[20]

Pickthall saw the word 'Muslim' not as a word describing the adherent of a creed, 'Islam', but as the Arabic word meaning 'one who surrenders totally' – to God. Pickthall's Islam was universal and comprehensive. Abraham was a Muslim and 'Jesus Christ will stand with us, the Muslims, on the Day of Judgment.'[21] For the Prophet Muhammad, a 'Unitarian Christian community would have been ... a Muslim community; and a Jewish community which rejected the priestcraft and superstition of the rabbis would have been the same.'[22] Indeed, a man may in some circumstances 'become a Muslim though he may not know it'.[23]

A perennial theme in Pickthall's religious writings was that salvation depended upon conduct: conduct, though not essential, is important for the Christian. 'Whosoever does right will be rewarded,' he preached in 1919, 'and whosoever does wrong will be punished, and no belief in any dogma will save him or her from the consequences which bad deeds entail.'[24] This article of faith allowed Pickthall a wide tolerance of outlook. 'In the Kingdom of Allah,' he told an audience six years later in Madras, 'there are no favourites. The Sacred Law is one for all, and non-Muslims who conform to it are more fortunate than professed Muslims who neglect or disobey its precepts.'[25] The conduct of a person covered all domains of life. It was 'the conduct of a man's whole life in every detail – man's conduct in relation to his brother man and to himself and to the animals and plants and all the life of earth'.[26]

For God was the author of all creation. His law was natural law. Before he became a Muslim Pickthall told a tale derived from al-Jabarti, the Egyptian chronicler of the occupation of Egypt by Napoleon's army. Napoleon wanted to cow the restless natives

'by sending up a big balloon with air in it. The people laughed at him. "Look," they said, "at that insignificant creature taking credit to himself for a thing he could never have done if God had not allowed!" For "God",' added Pickthall, 'read "natural laws discovered and discoverable or undiscoverable" and you will have a fair conception of the Moslem's faith. The European's pride in his inventions, and neglect to give the praise to God, shocks the Moslem at his best.'[27]

Islam encouraged scientific study of natural phenomena, for it revealed only the glory of God's work. In one of his first sermons he reflected on the devastation of Flanders. 'Man's most brutal efforts can change nothing of the natural laws. The grass will grow again on the battle-fields and wild flowers bloom upon the craters formed by bursting shells.'[28] The injunctions of the Prophet and of the Qur'an were also nothing more than exhortations to conform with natural law. For Pickthall the 'shari'ah is natural law. Those who follow it will succeed, and those who forsake it fail.'[29] The consequences of defying Islamic law are thus as unnatural as the consequences of defying gravity.

So much – belief in the overwhelming power of God, the need to surrender to his will, man's moral accountability and the natural law being seen as God's law – are religious principles that Pickthall was able to hold as a Christian or as a Muslim.

The second part of the *shahada*, declaring that Muhammad is the Prophet of God, is the point of divergence from Christianity.

Pickthall came 'to love him as one loves a friend'.[30] The Prophet had a 'sense of humour which was wise and genial'.[31] In spite of these qualities, however, he cannot claim the degree of reverence accorded by devout Christians to the person of Jesus Christ. The Prophet 'never claimed it, nor do Muslims claim it for him'.[32] In contrast to Jesus who proclaimed that his Kingdom was not of this world, the Prophet Muhammad clearly stressed the concerns of this world and prescribed rules for them.

It was this aspect of Islam which made it an advance on Christianity. Guidance on conduct in this world came from the Qur'an, from the authenticated sayings of the Prophet and from the *Sunna*, the received traditions of Islam. 'The Qur'ân repeatedly claims to be the confirmation of the truth of all religions.'[33] 'It is not upon the spiritual side that Christ's teaching in its original simplicity required supplementing, nor as regards the human side that it was incomplete . . . The Qur'ân completes the teaching of the Messiah by giving rules to be observed by true believers in such affairs as commerce, government, international politics, and war.'[34] The Prophet Muhammad laid the seal on any theological or moral development. Islam prescribes a body of obligations on matters of social and personal behaviour. Pickthall emphasized the importance of accepting these obligations. 'Religion means that which is binding on a man. Can anyone say that the teaching of Jesus of Nazareth is binding on Christians in the sense that the teaching of the Arab Prophet is binding on Muslims?'[35] These obligations were the declaration of the faith, the regular daily prayers, the giving of alms, the observance of the fast of Ramadan and the performance of the pilgrimage. In addition each Muslim is involved in a personal *jihad*. The *jihad* is not violent but a resolve to do better, to fight against the powers of evil, 'whether it be in his own conscience, or in the workshop, or in the market place, or in the council chamber or upon the battle-field'.[36]

Although in his religious writings Pickthall is generally addressing a Muslim readership – in the *Islamic Review* or the Madras lectures – he is often explaining and expounding Islam in terms of Western perceptions. He frequently writes about the need to distinguish Islamic precept (always good) from the practice of individual Muslims (sometimes bad). When he deals with something reprehensible in the practice of Muslims he criticizes it on Islamic grounds. But he also faces squarely objections made by westerners and Christians to Islam. In the course of his writings he deals frankly with free will, toleration, the institution of slavery, the position of women, and warfare.

Resignation to the will of God did not mean surrender of one's will or one's responsibility for initiative. For Pickthall, *jihad* was a very positive concept. He used to quote an Arabic proverb, 'Trust in God but tie your camel.'[37] The pursuit of wealth for its own sake or for selfish objectives was abhorrent to the spirit of Islam. But the obligation of *jihad* meant a constant striving for improvement, making an effort 'to assert and establish the sovereignty of God in men's minds, by performing his religious duty as laid down in the Qur'ân – an effort which should last through all his life, should govern every action of his life, or he is no true Muslim.'[38] Man has been endowed with free will to carry out this *jihad* and to show his adherence to God's laws by his conduct. Pickthall acknowledged that there is much fatalism in the teaching and practice of Muslims. But he sidestepped the philosophical question of predestination by saying that it was 'a question, like the definition of eternity, which is quite beyond our understanding – one of those matters which we are warned in the Qur'ân itself to let alone.'[39]

For European Christians tolerance is a secular virtue. But in Pickthall's view, tolerance was an obligation for Muslims.

Islam preaches equal justice to all men, tolerance for all sincere opinions, respect for all good men, wherever found ... I would urge most strongly on your notice the need to preach and practise ceaselessly this virtue of Islamic tolerance. We are forbidden to upset the wine of the non-Muslim. We are forbidden to speak anything concerning his religion which could hurt his feelings. The tolerance of Islam in history is our great claim to the consideration of the world. The tolerance of Islam in the future may heal the wounds of humanity.[40]

The Prophet, by emphasizing moral conduct minimized the significance of confessional belief. Consequently, religious tolerance 'is the very essence of Islam. The Qur'ân enjoins it, and Muhammad in his life as Prophet and as ruler showed how it could be practised both in war and peace. He it was who first announced in terms which no one can misconstrue that Allah rewards the good of every creed and nation.' Nonetheless Muslims had, Pickthall recognized, been guilty of intolerance. This was not right. 'No; when we do so we belie our faith.'[41]

But he went on to define limits to tolerance. 'Evil is not equal with good, and evil where it shows its head must be repressed, and sternly.'[42] On the other hand he drew attention to the many favourable instances of Islamic tolerance, above all in the freedom extended to Christian communities. When Christendom in turn has become tolerant, it is following an Islamic policy. 'The civil law of England is today more Islamic in its equal justice to all creeds and races than is the practice of old-fashioned Muslims.'[43] Tolerance is an aid to success. When Muslims have been distinguished by personal righteousness, for simple faith and for tolerance, they have been politically most successful. And there is a contrast between Christendom's repressive attitude towards dissidents and minorities and Islam's regularized treatment of Christian communities.

In several of his later novels Pickthall describes the status of slaves in Islamic countries. The household they are in treats slaves with affection. Many of slave origin in Islamic history have achieved distinction. The central character of *Knights of Araby* (1917) is a king from a slave background. Islam sanctioned the enslavement of captives in warfare, but the Prophet commanded that they be clothed and fed. 'The slave was regarded as a son or daughter of the house, and in default of heirs inherited the property.'[44] Manumission was a meritorious act. 'The slave-trade was a horror which had no Islamic sanction. I do not say that there were no abuses in the Muslim world, but I do say that they were not what Europeans have imagined, and have no analogy with things similarly named in Christendom.'[45]

Marmaduke Pickthall's father, the Rev. Charles Grayson Pickthall, from
family photographs belonging to the late Mrs Dorothy Rudkin, reproduced
by permission of Dr Robert Pacey.

Marmaduke Pickthall's mother, Mrs Mary Pickthall, from family
photographs belonging to the late Mrs Dorothy Rudkin, reproduced by
permission of Dr Robert Pacey.

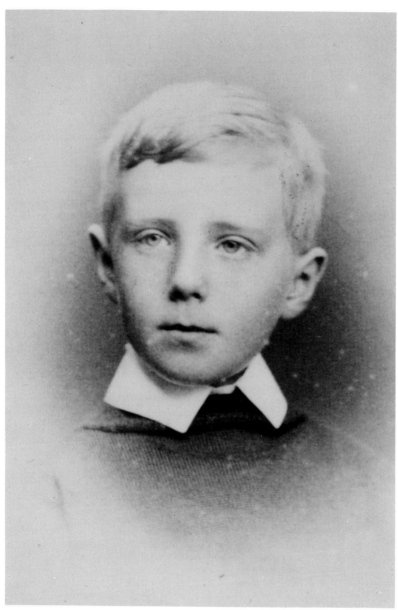
Marmaduke Pickthall as a boy, from family photographs belonging to the late Mrs Dorothy Rudkin, reproduced by permission of Dr Robert Pacey.

Chillesford Rectory in about 1930 from a photograph reproduced by permission of Mrs Mary Snell.

Marmaduke Pickthall towards the end of his life from *Islamic Culture*, 1936.

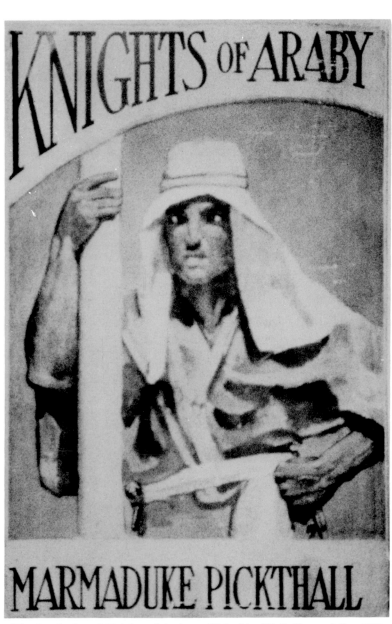

The dust jacket of *Knights of Araby*, published by W. Collins and Co., 1917.
Photograph by Studio Vedette, Tunis.

Chadarghat High School for Boys, Hyderabad, in 1985. Photograph by Photo Capital, Hyderabad.

Marmaduke Pickthall's grave at Brookwood Cemetery, Surrey, in 1985.
Photograph by Mike Stammers, Photo Services, Woking.

Pickthall, like many commentators on Islam, gave much attention to the role of women. Several sermons and articles dealt with the matter. It was the central theme of one of his novels, a minor and recurrent theme in others. The preoccupation was defensive. In Islamic countries, men wield a monopoly of authority, power and resources which is not significantly modified by Qur'anic prescriptions for the regulation of property. Indeed the defining of limited rights for women legitimizes and perpetuates the bias towards patriarchal authority – especially as it is men who define those rights.[46] In his novels Pickthall recognizes awful injustices that spring from this inequality. He is sensitive to women's rights but the wrongs arise from human sinfulness rather than from Islam. In 1919 he wrote on 'The Position of Women in Islam'. Eight years later a lecture with much of the same content is more tactfully called 'The Relations of the Sexes': a significant shift of emphasis.

'The Prophet of Islam,' said Pickthall more than once, 'was perhaps the greatest feminist the world has ever known, considering the country and the age in which he lived.'[47] In the seventh century women in Arabia had to put up with much degradation and baby girls were sometimes buried alive. But the Prophet regulated the situation of women. He protected their rights and their property and pressed for their education. Wife-beating was condemned. Women's dignity was upheld. 'Muhammad found a system of unbounded licence for the lusts of men, and made of it a decorous social order.'[48] 'Women have equal rights with men before the Sharî'ah, and the Qu'rân proclaims that they are equal with men in the sight of God.'[49]

The exploitation of women has no justification in Islam. 'There is no text in the Qu'rân, no saying of our Prophet, which can possibly be held to justify the practice of depriving women of the natural benefits which Allah has decreed for all mankind – sunshine and fresh air and healthy movement – or her life-long imprisonment causing the death by consumption or anaemia of thousands of women every year; and God knows how many babies.'[50] In his Madras lectures, Pickthall deplores the status accorded to Muslim women. She 'is emphatically *not* in her Islamic position . . . The status to which the great majority of Muslim women in India are reduced is a libel on Islam, a crime.'[51]

Women were equal in the spiritual sphere and should be equal before the law.

And in the temporal sphere what does the inequality amount to? A frank admission of the fact that woman is the weaker sex, and that in a state of society where men are violent they must be protected by strict laws, and some seclusion. The law of El Islam in this and many other matters is not static, as some people suppose, but dynamic; not stringent, but elastic enough to comprehend the needs of every age and every people.[52]

A frequent point made by Pickthall is that western literature sentimentalizes women. They are treated as objects of chivalry. Marriage is regarded as the primary goal of women. Pickthall argued that Muslim women were not sentimental in their approach to marriage. If love accompanied a marriage arranged by families as if it were a legal contract, then that love was a bonus. The Muslim women in *Veiled Women* (1913) and *The House of War* (1916) surprise their western sisters by the breadth of their education and the freedom of their conversation. He told a congregation of 1919 that the Muslim women he knew 'discussed quite freely subjects which would make the venerable Mrs Grundy's hair stand on end. They thought of death and birth and all realities quite calmly and naturally.'[53]

For Pickthall marriage was an unsentimental business. It was an illusion to imagine

> that there can be a perfect union of two human souls . . . The wife is a free servant of Allah, and so is the husband. Their relationship is clearly regulated by the sacred law. Beyond that regulation they preserve their own opinions, their own thoughts. Each serves Allah, but in a different way. That seems to me a nobler and more sensible ideal than one which strives to tear away the veils of personality, seeking a communion which is quite impossible, and attaining an intimacy which is more likely to prove disastrous than satisfactory.[54]

This chilly view of marriage hints at a personal loneliness. The same point of view was expressed with eloquent passion in three novels written around the time that he embraced Islam – *Veiled Women*, *Knights of Araby* (1917) and *The Early Hours* (1921).

In Pickthall's view, Islam scored over Christianity with its precepts for dealing with the unpleasant aspects of this world. The otherworldliness of Christianity was escapist. Conflict and warfare were facts of life, arising out of human nature. The Prophet, by both example and teaching, legislated for warfare.

The Prophet did not love war. He started his career pacifically. When he was in a tight corner he would sooner seek terms than take up arms. For long he adopted a Christian attitude on non-resistance. 'It was only when his enemies were actually in the field against him, advancing with the avowed design to hound him down in El

Medinah, to destroy his people, and exterminate Islam, that the command was given to the Muslims to take part in war.' Many of his supporters protested that it was not right to resist aggression. 'It was only by the weight of a new revelation from on high that their objections . . . were overcome.'[55] Henceforth fighting became a duty. Nonetheless the Prophet imposed severe limitations on the conduct of warfare. He never himself practised those severe measures of warfare that the Qur'an allows, 'thereby showing that such severity was to be used only in the last extremity to stop abominations which could not be checked by other means'.[56] Open enemies were treated more leniently than false allies. 'Before Muhammad's time – and among non-Muslims for centuries after his time; aye, even to the present day – the fact of one set of people being captured by another meant that the conquered forfeited all human rights and lay entirely at the mercy of the conqueror, even though they might be of the same religion.'[57] The Prophet changed all that. The vanquished had rights, and as far as Islamic security permitted, were allowed to conduct their own affairs. Economic weapons were forbidden. Quiet folk, including folk of other religions, were not to be molested. Means of livelihood were not to be destroyed. He even forbad those loans at favourable rates, that may raise funds for combatants. 'We are commanded to give it, when the State is risking its existence on the hazard of war. That command makes short work of the profiteer.'[58]

In sum, Christianity ignores war and Islam regulates it.

Pickthall saw in Islam a community of believers that transcended class and race – and even time. 'Personal ambition, national ambition, tribal jealousy – all the passions which compose what we call patriotism – he [the Prophet Muhammad] abjured as criminal. Instead he preached the brotherhood of believers.'[59] He envisaged the ideal Islamic society 'where men, both rich and poor, in full accord with custom and with law, are able to serve God in spirit and in truth, have leisure to develop their full personality, and try to help their neighbours, not to get the better of them'.[60] Islamic worship is timeless. Go to Sultan Hasan mosque in Cairo, Pickthall observed in 1919, go to al-Aqsa mosque in Jerusalem, visit 'any of the great cathedrals of Islam – or go into some little mud-built village mosque in Central Africa, everywhere it is the same service; there has been no alteration, no elaboration since the Prophet's day.'[61] As an Englishman he saw in Islam an emancipation from class prejudice. He recognized that class distinctions and great inequalities existed but he found that a Muslim's 'vision grows serene, enabling him to smile at the pretensions of all parties, to accept men on their merits, with a brotherly regard for men whose conduct pleases him irrespective of class or race or colour.'[62]

In the community of believers was to be found a spirit of fraternity. Of the other catchwords of nineteenth-century liberalism, liberty and equality were to Pickthall ideals, abstract and unobtainable. Fraternity, on the other hand, was 'personal, and can be realized wherever men of the like conscience and good will consort together.'[63] Pickthall, as a man of conscience and good will, succeeded in forging a fraternity with Syrians, Egyptians, Turks and Indians as well as like-minded Englishmen.

Some aspects of Pickthall's Islam were more personal, even idiosyncratic. They were a reflection of his own background in a post-Darwinian England or of a Victorian ethic for which some features of Islam struck a chord. Four such features that a cradle Muslim would not have stressed were: assets as a trust; the role of quiet people; spiritualism; and sentimentality.

Property was trust. There was no merit in the pursuit of wealth. Simple 'selfish strife for gain does not appeal to him [the Muslim] as worthy of sustained endeavour. It is, indeed, unlawful in the brotherhood of Islam.'[64] A man should never 'become so absorbed in his temporal possessions or occupations that it would break his heart to be deprived of them.'[65] Private property extended even to the limbs of your person. On one occasion he contrasted what he saw as a Christian approval of self-mutilation ('If thine eye offend thee, pluck it out') with the Islamic concept of trust: as 'if our eyes, our hands, our feet, were ours alone, to deal with as we liked, as if they did not in a sense belong to all mankind'.[66] Property was to be used for the pursuit of *jihad* and not to be used to exploit the needy. 'We have to spend what God has given us, not only money but all other gifts, in God's way, not our own way . . . after you have satisfied your needs and the needs of those dependent on you, have paid your poor rate, and bestowed a due amount in charity' – you spend the rest, 'spend it in such a way as directly to benefit your fellow men, to encourage the deserving, and increase the sense of human brotherhood'.[67]

Pickthall often wrote of 'the quiet people' – sometimes scholars and teachers, usually unambitious ordinary farmers. Frequently the main people of his novels are unheroic and are contrasted with the powerful who erred in involving quiet people in his personal disputes.

A ruler wishing to make war upon another ruler must do so at his personal expense, with the help of slaves bought with his own money and such others as might join him of their own free will. He and his army must not touch the life or occupation of the peaceful Muslims. Any wrong done to the peaceful Muslims – 'the quiet people', as they called them, was punished by the 'Ulama, who could rouse the whole Muslim world against the delinquent. So such wars did practically no injury whatever to the civilization or solidarity of the Muslims.[68]

Pickthall claimed that, in times when the Caliphate was weak and lacked control, this is what actually happened. 'The quiet people went about their work as usual. They stood and watched the glittering hosts of fighting slaves go by to battle somewhere with some other host of fighting slaves. They watched the pageant with a shrug of the shoulders and a prayer that sinful men might be forgiven, and they went on calmly with their work.'[69] *Knights of Araby* is a novel about conflicts between ambitious rulers. The quiet people of Zabid gaze on for ever inclining prudently to the men in power, even though they harboured specific loyalties in their hearts.

Pickthall was interested in psychical research. For him, any scientific research was acceptable to Muslims for it simply revealed more of the natural laws, more of the laws of God. There were no limits to enquiry and the speculations of the spiritualists should in no way be shunned. In spite of hostility, spiritualism had, he wrote in an article for *Islamic Culture* in 1927, gained ground. 'It is really nothing new except as regards phraseology and was perfectly familiar to the gnostic Christians of old, a remnant of whom found a refuge from the church's persecution in Islam and perpetuated their ideas among the Sûfis.'[70] Pickthall thought that, taking into consideration spiritualism's premises and applying its tests 'so far as we are able, we come to the conclusion that the whole Qurân-ush-Sharif is a "communication", or rather a long connected series of "communications" from the other world.'[71] Psychical research should not be derided; its conclusions should not be denied. It was all a confirmation of the Qur'anic text – ' "Say not of those who are slain in the way of Allah (that they are) dead, but living, only ye do not perceive."'[72] Modern western spiritualists now accepted, in contrast to scientists of the 1870s, the idea of miracles, though they limited their acceptance to the miraculous element in the Bible. But, in Pickthall's view, 'they have come near the Muslim theory of Prophethood'.[73]

An awareness of natural laws, God's laws, led to an unsentimental approach to life. Repeatedly in his novels and in his sermons Pickthall rejects 'sentimentality', seeing it as a western failure. Sentimentality ranges from a romantic flabby attitude to the relationship between the sexes to a flight from reality, a preference for abstractions rather than reality. 'You cannot be a

Muslim and a sentimentalist. For nature has no sentimentality, and Muslims reverence the laws of nature as the laws of God.'[74] Hence Muslims do not, or should not, retreat from the world. Islam exhorts the believer to involve himself in communal activity, to face the grim reality of warfare and death.

4.

THE SERVANT OF ISLAM:
INDIA, THE QUR'AN

'I suppose the same destruction of romance and
installation of Jazz is going on all over the world
except in dear old Hyderabad.'

Pickthall in 1929[1]

Pickthall's conversion to Islam coincided with the defeat of Turkey at
the end of the First World War, followed by the collapse of the
Ottoman Empire. The position claimed by the Ottoman Sultans since
the eighteenth century of 'successors' to the authority handed down
from the Prophet Muhammad himself was abolished by Mustafa
Kemal, the leader of the new Turkey. In 1923, the question of the
'khalifa' or 'successor' was already a vibrant issue in many countries
with Muslim majorities and minorities, and especially in India.

In 1774 the Treaty of Küçük Kaynarca had legitimized Russia's
sovereignty over the Crimea. The Czar also had certain rights of
intervention in the Ottoman Empire on behalf of orthodox Christians. In response and in compensation, the Turkish Sultan made a
new claim. Tartar Muslims were to owe him allegiance according to
the prescriptions of their religion.[2] At this time in Turkey there
appeared for the first time the legend of how the last of the 'Abbasid
Caliphs transferred his khilafa to the Sultan Selim I in 1517.[3]

It was however a century later that the Sultan Abdul Hamid II used
modern technology – the telegraph and the press – to assert the
claims of the khilafa and to hint at authority over all Muslims. He
patronized Muslims from all over the world and sent his own agents

in all directions. Emissaries canvassed support for him in Africa, Egypt and India. In the 1880s a newspaper was published under his patronage in Istanbul edited by a Punjabi who had been dismissed from the Indian government service. It attacked British rule in India.[4]

In India, Abdul Hamid's ideological expansionism met a sympathetic response. After the Mutiny the Mughal Emperor, for long ineffective, was exiled to Burma and a focal point of Islamic authority was removed. Some of the leading Muslims looked westward and, following the example of Sayyid Ahmad Khan, took to wearing the fez, a symbol of nineteenth-century Turkey.[5] Prayers in Indian mosques were frequently offered to the Ottoman Sultan. The British did not discourage these sentiments. Islamic loyalty to the Sultan was stressed to the Indian troops brought to the Mediterranean in 1877 as a deterrent to Russian advances towards the Turkish capital.

By the turn of the century the authority of the *khilafa* and concern for Ottoman reputation were widespread among Islamic communities. The Greco-Turkish war of 1897 led to stirrings or outbreaks in India, Madagascar, Turkestan and the East Indies as well as in India. In 1913 the radical pan-Islamic Indian educationalist and writer, Muhammad 'Ali, through his journal, *Comrade,* organized relief for the Turks in the Balkan campaigns and reported fully tales of Christian atrocities.

There was thus no strangeness in Pickthall's shifting his political interests from Turkey to India after the First World War. During the war he came into regular contact with young Muslims, mainly from India, who worshipped at the mosque in London. In 1919 Pickthall was involved with an Islamic Information Bureau which produced a weekly journal, the *Muslim Outlook,* as well as information on the Turkish defence of Anatolia. In the words of a police report this propaganda 'endeavoured to keep before the public exaggerated accounts of the atrocities committed by the Greeks in Smyrna and to cause apprehension by declaring that the Muslim world was in a state of frenzy owing to the threatened dismemberment of the Ottoman Empire'.[6]

In early 1920 Muhammad 'Ali came to England to urge the cause of the *khilafa* upon the British government. The government cold-shouldered Muhammad 'Ali and his delegation but Pickthall was in touch with him and hosted a dinner party on 19 February.[7]

In 1920 Pickthall was in need of money, a job and security. The *Bombay Chronicle* was a journal whose aim was to further the cause of Indian progress. In 1920 its editor, Benjamin Guy Horniman, was deported to Ceylon, and the Board of Management of the newspaper invited Pickthall, now well known in India, to succeed him. He was offered 1,400 rupees a month as salary and negotiated a probationary period of six months.

After sending off to the publisher, Collins, his last novel, the *Early Hours*, Pickthall set sail for India in September 1920. India was to become his home for the next fifteen years. His time there can be divided into two unequal parts, the first four years in Bombay and the years 1925–35 when he was based in Hyderabad.

The Pickthalls landed at Bombay and stayed at the Taj Mahal Hotel. Marmaduke was welcomed by Muslims and by the Bombay Khilafat Committee. The work of editing the newspaper was time-consuming and exhausting. He had to face labour problems and to manage people as he had never had to before. His life was decidedly with Indians and he faced something of a boycott from the British community. Pickthall did not care too much 'as I meet much more interesting folk'.[8] But Muriel was not happy and when Pickthall took his first home leave she came to England and did not return to India for two years. He recognized that India owed a lot to England. Indeed ideas of liberty and of a unified India were derived from Britain. India, he wrote for the *Islamic Review* in 1921, 'was asleep, and it is now awake. The very animosity which nowadays I hear expressed against the very thought of foreign rule, the bare idea of India – that half-continent – as a nation having rights and personality, is the result of English teaching.'[9]

While he was busy with his paper, Pickthall had ample time to get involved in political and religious activities. During 1921 Gandhi was creating a bridge between the Hindu and Muslim communities by giving support to the Khilafat movement. Pickthall was close to Gandhi during this year and shared platforms with him. Pickthall saw Gandhi as 'a saint and an angel – anything you like in that way – but the most obstinate little man who ever walked this earth. I love him and believe that he will revive India, but his autocratic tone makes enemies.'[10] Pickthall presided at a Khilafat Conference in Sind in July 1921 and acknowledged the leadership of a Hindu over an Islamic movement. In this acknowledgement he was applying his religious view that conduct, regardless of nominal confessional loyalty, was the supreme test. 'I think that a Hindu saint who lives upon the higher plane is a better guide for Muslims than a Muslim sinner who lives upon the lower plane, for upon the higher plane there is but one law for Muslims, Hindus, Christians, Jews or any man and that law is the divine law revealed in the Qurân-e-Sharif.'[11]

Pickthall was invited to Muslim communities throughout India. He preached in the mosque at Bijapur and lectured at the Islamic University at Aligarh. In 1922 he travelled to eastern India, to Muzafferpur. He took up the study of Urdu.

The Board of the *Bombay Chronicle* appreciated the value of Pickthall and his contract was renewed each year until 1924. In the autumn of 1921 he came to Europe on leave for the winter months. He prepared a collection of short stories for Collins who published them under the title *As Others See Us* in 1922, and returned to India via France and Egypt. In Paris he called on Yusuf Kemal, the head of a delegation from Ankara and in Port Said he saw 'at the landing-stage an elderly lieutenant in the uniform of the Suez Canal Police and, after staring at him for a minute, went up and asked whether his name was not Rashid'.[12] It was and it turned out to be the discharged Ottoman soldier who had accompanied Pickthall in Syria in the 1890s.

During the 1920s Pickthall published two short stories with Indian themes. They were the last fiction he published though he worked on a novel based on the Moghal Empire, *Dust and the Peacock Throne*. Both short stories were published in the *Cornhill Magazine* in London and one was republished in the *Best Short Stories of 1925*.

Both stories are tales of Indian students and their search for the truth. Both describe scenes of India in his characteristically circumstantial way. In 'The Quest' he describes a shop by a wide road. A splendid baobab tree stood near 'a species of pavilion in which all sorts of people took their ease. There was a barber on a strip of carpet shaving the hair beneath a peasant's armpits.'[13] Pickthall came to love India but his love, like that for the Arabs of Syria, was not distorted by false romanticism or sentimentality. The students of the stories are involved in the nationalist movement and we see the police and English institutions through the eyes of Hindu Indian nationalists of an unexalted class. The British appear but are unimportant to the stories. An observation by one of the students that the English 'rank athletic powers above learning'[14] is the only instance where Pickthall's own values obtrude.

Pickthall's own views were presented regularly in the *Bombay Chronicle*. He also sent articles to England on matters that roused him. When Mustafa Kemal (later Atatürk) abolished the caliphate (the *khilafa*) Pickthall took it all very philosophically. It was better, he wrote in the *Islamic Review* in 1923, for the *khilafa* no longer to be narrowly and contentiously 'identified with a military despotism, nor with the political ambitions of a single country. It is for us, the Muslims, to make it once more what it ought to be, the standard of Islam, a faithful witness to the greater Khilafat – the viceroyalty of man to God – showing mankind only the way of human progress.'[15] At the end of his life he thought the *khilafa* movement that had once seemed so strong had been 'suddenly deflated' by Atatürk's action.[16] In 1924 he wrote of India in the *Islamic Review*. Communal violence had recently broken out in the State of Hyderabad. There had, according to Pickthall,been no trouble until 1924. He attributed the strife to the spontaneous growth of a movement 'which sprang up in British India after the removal of Mahatma Gandhi's humanizing and restraining influence'.[17] And in 1925 he wrote in E.D. Morel's radical journal, *Foreign Affairs,* protesting against British intervention in the Gulf state of Bahrain.

In late 1924 the *Bombay Chronicle* was sold. The new management wanted Pickthall to take a line hostile to Gandhi and he refused. Pickthall and the paper parted company and he was obliged to look for a job.

During his four years in Bombay Pickthall had developed a close friendship with Captain W.E. Gladstone Solomon, an art historian of South African origin. Solomon was Principal of the School of Art and for a time Pickthall lived at the School in the house where Rudyard Kipling was born. Solomon was an historian of Moghul art and Pickthall became greatly interested in the independent Islamic empire of India that became gradually eroded as the British advanced in the eighteenth and nineteenth centuries. Many Indian states that had been allies or offshoots of the Moghul Empire evaded absorption into the British Empire and preserved a nominal independence in contrast to 'British India'. The largest of these states was the Nizamate of Hyderabad.

Pickthall wanted to work for the Nizam in some capacity and two senior ministers of the Nizam offered him first the principalship of Osmania University. This fell through but he was appointed Principal of Chadarghat High School for Boys.

Pickthall arrived in Hyderabad in January 1925. The next ten years were in many ways the happiest of his life. Hyderabad was then a city of 400,000 inhabitants on the southern bank of the Musi River. It was the capital of the State which had a population in 1925 of twelve million. Although the ruling family were Muslims, the vast majority of the subjects were not. The Nizam had been the ruler since 1911 and was a patron of Arabs – from the Hadramaut in particular – and of Islamic scholarship. In 1924 Pickthall wrote that it was 'in Hyderabad that the conditions of the Moghul Empire are most accurately reproduced today, for it is a fragment of that Empire which survived the general ruin'.[18] The Nizam enjoyed great prestige among Muslims all over India and also among Hindus for his government's officials were recruited from the whole of India – and beyond. The Nizam's government was tolerant and contributed towards the construction of Hindu temples. Communal problems were those of all India but in Hyderabad, Pickthall wrote in 1936, 'they have hitherto been solved quite happily by the old Moghul attitude of tolerance'.[19]

The Nizam himself, His Exalted Highness Sir Usman Ali Khan Bahadur, was a poet in Persian and Urdu. Pickthall's conservatism and monarchism was soothed by the very benevolent despotism of the Nizam. The town and the state had seen many developments in its public services in the Nizam's reign and Pickthall saw an Islamic ideal polity in operation. Islam was demonstrably – necessarily – tolerant. Islamic traditions and teaching prescribed the rules of political behaviour and it was within these rules that the Nizam's government worked. These rules included precepts for dealing with non-Muslims and there was thus no paradox in a largely Hindu state being governed by a Muslim.

Hyderabad was a cultural centre and Pickthall thought in 1931 that it 'may soon become the chief cultural centre in India'.[20] It also became a centre of the Urdu language, a language that Pickthall took pains to learn. Urdu was the language of the Osmania University founded by the Nizam and named after him. With this foundation, at a stroke, he 'made Hyderabad the undisputed capital of Urdu'.[21] A translation bureau was active translating scientific texts into Urdu, a language which – Pickthall claimed in 1928 – had two hundred million speakers.[22]

Pickthall was a headmaster for three years. It was another new role for him, in addition to which he became responsible for training prospective civil servants for the Hyderabad Civil Service. In Civil Service House he built up the library and selected its books – but did not choose his own works. He taught European literature to his students. One former student, Mohammed Shafiuddin, recalls how he made *Don Quixote* 'more interesting and amusing when he performed the action of tilting at the windmills like Don Quixote'.[23] Pupils recall his piety and the meticulous performance of his religious obligations. He used to have very little time to himself. He was reserved, friendly and modest to his students. Another former student, Hameeduddin Ahmed recollects that the students 'had little chance of breaking Hazrat Pickthall's calculated silence about himself. We met him and Mrs Pickthall each night at dinner which usually lasted about an hour and a half. The talk was mostly about matters of topical interest; enlivened always with the inimitable humour and pleasant conversation of Hazrat Pickthall.'[24]

In taking up his duties in Hyderabad Pickthall was obliged to eschew political activities, but as the years went by he became employed more and more by the Nizam on confidential matters separate from his formal educational duties. He became a courtier. In 1930 he was in England and acted as secretary to the Hyderabad delegation at the Round Table Conference. The following year he squired a son of the Nizam on a visit to Europe. At Nice in November the son married Princess Dürrühesvar, daughter of the last of the Caliphs, Sultan Abdul-mecid II. And in the early 1930s he was made Controller to a younger relation of the Nizam, Sahibzada Basalat Jung, acting as it would seem as a kind of tutor-companion.

But the most important work Pickthall did during his Hyderabad years consisted of the tasks he undertook for the sake of Islam.

In 1925 he was invited by a Committee of Muslims in Madras to deliver a series of lectures on the cultural side of Islam. The first lecture was delivered in October 1925 and the series was published in 1927. The lectures present Islam in a way that is most acceptable for non-Muslims. They reveal a clarity of expression and are a straightforward but nonetheless individualistic summary of his own beliefs. Familiar themes come forward – the importance of personal conduct, progress, the depressed status of women especially in India, the need for a reformed Islam and informed Muslims.

Two years later he became editor of *Islamic Culture*, a new quarterly journal produced under the patronage of the Nizam. The journal was in English and contained articles by authorities both Muslim and non-Muslim of a high academic standard. Under the ten years of Pickthall's editorship there were articles by old acquaintances like George Hornblower and W.E. Gladstone Solomon, established academics like D.S. Margoliouth, and by younger scholars and orientalists like Muhammad Asad (Leopold Weiss), Muhammad Hamidullah and Freya Stark. In each number Pickthall usually reviewed half a dozen books on an extraordinary range of subjects. He reviewed the state of Islamic studies in Spanish. He commented about books that had been written in German, French, Italian, Persian and Urdu. He wrote about Islamic history, Semitic linguistics, Indian music, cancer, and spiritualism. His articles are a useful critical source of literature published in Urdu and English in India on Islamic studies. Among the books reviewed were an early book on Turkic dialects by Gunnar Jarring, Lady Evelyn Cobbold's account of her pilgrimage to Mecca and T.E. Lawrence's *Seven Pillars of Wisdom*. He encouraged the writing, both scholarly and creative, of Indian writers but was something of a critical martinet, being fastidious about transliteration. Scholars 'do not want to know how words are pronounced in any country but how they are spelt'.[25] Sometimes his recent career as a schoolmaster peeps through. He is pleased by a work that has been produced by the University of Madras. 'Especially we must praise the careful and correct transliteration – rare in India – which proves, if proof were needed, the translator's scholarship. The printing and get-up are excellent. Only occasionally in the English we happen on an unfamiliar word or idiom, as for instance the translator's use of 'horses' when he means cavalry. In English we see 'horse' (——soldiers understood) and 'foot' (—— soldiers understood).'[26] And from time to time we have a bit of donnish humour. 'To the leaflet of Errata we should like to add: "For Eratta read Errata"; but such are the vicissitudes of Indian printing.'[27]

As editor Pickthall was in touch with scholarly Muslims all over the world. 'Our Hyderabad,' he recalled a few months before he died, 'is a sort of capital for all Muslims. All kinds of people come there from afar, attracted by the fabled wealth of His Exalted Highness. And many of them used to call on me at my office, or greet me in the mosque, and tell me things.'[28]

In 1928 the Nizam gave Pickthall special leave of absence on full pay for two years in order to complete his translation of the Qur'an. This is the work for which he has been best known during the last fifty years, and which he considered as the summit of his own life's work. It was the first translation by a Muslim whose first language was English. Other translations were, as he wrote in 1919, by 'Arabic scholars, preoccupied by individual words which present difficulties, rather than by the meaning as a whole'.[29]

According to Muslims, the Qur'an is the word of God and as such cannot be translated. Pickthall maintained this himself and in his foreword wrote: 'The Qur'an cannot be translated. That is the belief of old-fashioned sheykhs and the view of the present writer.'[30] The title of the work he finally published in 1930 was *The Meaning of the Glorious Koran*. It is the rendering in English of the message, a *sura* by *sura* presentation in English of the Arabic text. In a similar way, A.J. Arberry more recently called his translation, *The Koran Interpreted*.

The work of 'translating' the Qur'an had been in Pickthall's mind since he embraced Islam. Before that declaration he thought all the translations were 'prosaic explanations'.[31] Shortly after his declaration he preached on the Qur'an in an address on the Prophet's birthday. 'The book is like no other book on earth. Explanations of the mystery of its existence have been suggested by the sceptical but none explains it. It remains a wonder of the world.'[32] Pickthall himself, who found 'great dificulty in remembering well-known English quotations accurately' found he could 'remember page after page of the Qur'an in Arabic with perfect accuracy'.[33] In 1919 he elaborated his feelings of the miraculous nature of the Book and the danger of adoring editions rather than the contents. 'Beware how you pay veneration to the book itself, the letters and the binding and the form of words, for that way lies idolatry and death. But keep the message always in your hearts, and live by it.'[34]

When he was Acting Imam in London in 1919 Pickthall was not

satisfied with the published translations he used. So he put them to one side 'and made my own translation of any passage which I wished to read out in English'.[35] In other sermons and addresses and writings he frequently used his own translation of texts. But it was the stimulus of living among Muslims in India that urged him to translate the whole work. He was aware of the different approach to the book by Arabs and non-Arabs. Pickthall saw that there was an obligation for all Muslims to know the Qur'an intimately. Pickthall's ally in the Khilafat movement, Muhammad 'Ali, had already produced a translation. Such work was in no way to be regarded as a substitute. 'No non-Arab Muslims, so far as I know,' wrote Pickthall, 'ever had the least idea of elevating a translation of the Scripture in their language to the position of the English translation of the Bible among English speaking Protestant Christians.'[36]

By 1927 he was actively engaged in translating and during his leave from Hyderabad consulted scholars in Europe. As a conscientious traditional Muslim he wanted to secure approval from the most learned authority of the world of Islam, the *'ulama* of al-Azhar in Cairo. And in 1928 Lord Lloyd, then High Commissioner in Egypt (and formerly Governor of Bombay), met Pickthall in London and arranged for him to go to Egypt and consult the Azhar scholars.

Pickthall was in Egypt for three months from November 1929. He was furnished with a letter of introduction to Shaykh Mustafa al-Maraghi who had been the Rector of al-Azhar already and was to occupy that position again. He had two other main alies in Egypt. One was Fuad Salim al-Hijazi, who had been Turkish Ambassador to Switzerland during the war and was an old acquaintance of Pickthall. The other was Muhammad Ahmad al-Ghamrawi, a chemist at the University of Cairo and an authority on early Arabic literature.

Pickthall's scruples created difficulties for him. To ask permission invites the option of that permission being refused. The less scrupulous do not face such problems. In Cairo at that time Pickthall saw two translations of the Qur'an by non-Muslims on sale in bookshops, 'one of them having on its paper jacket a picture representing our Prophet and the angel Gabriel'[37]; such representations were universally deplored by Muslims.

During his sojourn in Egypt Pickthall met many of the leading Egyptian writers of the day. Ahmad Lutfi al-Sayyid hosted a meeting of four Azhari scholars who would go over Pickthall's text. Rashid Rida gave Pickthall his backing. Taha Husayn, the blind professor of Arabic at the secular University of Cairo, told Pickthall that King Fuad of Egypt, 'had somehow been impressed with the idea that translation of the Qur'ân was sinful',[38] and that he might also dismiss from al-Azhar any who aided Pickthall. If true, the King's objections are strange. He posed as an Islamic leader, even toying with the idea of assuming the *khilafa*, the caliphate, himself.[39] Yet he lacked mastery in Arabic.[40] Pickthall found Taha Husayn tiresome and obstructive, even more so when the latter proposed that Pickthall should approach the King to get a *fatwa* approving the work of translation. Pickthall coolly pointed out that he already had a *fatwa*, from India, and as for royal patronage, he was fully supported by the Nizam of Hyderabad.

Pickthall persevered and worked through his translation with scholars and secured their approval. But a report of his task reached the daily paper, *Al-Ahram*, and a former professor at al-Azhar, Shaykh Muhammad Shakir, wrote an article denouncing Pickthall, his work and his collaborators. It would be more meritorious, wrote the Shaykh, if the Islamic commentaries of Tabari were translated. Pickthall's reaction was that many Egyptian views were curiously insular. He wrote afterwards that

> many Egyptian Muslims were as surprised as I was at the extraordinary ignorance of present world conditions of men who claimed to be thinking of the needs of the Islamic world – men who think that the Arabs are still 'the patrons', and the non-Arabs their 'freedmen'; who cannot see that the positions have become reversed, that the Arabs are no longer the fighters and the non-Arabs the stay-at-homes but it is the non-Arabs who at present bear the brunt of the Jihad; that the problems of the non-Arabs are not identical with those of the Arabs; that translation of the Qur'ân is for the non-Arabs a necessity which, of course, it is not for the Arabs; men who cannot conceive that there are Muslims in India as learned and devout, as capable of judgement and as careful for the safety of Islam, as any to be found in Egypt.[41]

He left Egypt in March 1930 and *The Meaning of the Glorious Koran* was published by A.A. Knopf of New York in December 1930. The following year Pickthall learnt that the Rector of al-Azhar was not happy with the translation after all. 'The latest rumour', Pickthall heard from Muhammad Ahmad al-Ghamrawi, 'was that Al-Azhar had decided that the whole work must be translated word for word back into Arabic and submitted to their judgement in that distorted form, as none of the professors could read English.' Pickthall feared that this was likely 'to bring a degree of ridicule upon Al-Azhar, which I should be the first to deplore'. Later, a press cutting informed him that 'after examining my work in the distorted form already mentioned, the Rector of Al-Azhar had pronounced it, "though the best of all translations" unfit to be authorized in Egypt. The reason given for the ban is that I have translated idiomatic and metaphorical Arabic phrases literally into English, thus showing that I have not understood their real meaning.'[42]

Muhammad 'Ali's translation had been condemned outright. Pickthall consoled himself with the reflection that the position that all translation was sinful had been abandoned. A 'translation of the Qur'ân by a Muslim has been examined and a literary reason has been given for its condemnation. That,' he concluded sardonically, 'is a great step forward.'[43]

Pickthall was not to forget what he thought was Taha Husayn's obstruction. In 1925 Taha Husayn published a book, *Fi'l Shi'r al-Jahili* (On Pre-Islamic Poetry) in which he questioned the authenticity of pre-Islamic poetry. In the same year the Professor of Arabic of the University of Oxford, D.S. Margoliouth, published a monograph in the *Journal of the Royal Asiatic Society*, expressing identical ideas. There is no evidence that Taha Husayn had borrowed the ideas. Taha Husayn's book caused a public scandal and he withdrew it from the market. Among those who repudiated his arguments was Muhammad Ahmad al-Ghamrawi. Taha Husayn had applied modern methods of textual criticism to ancient poetry. Such an approach, if applied to the texts of religion, might appear to question the divine origin of the Qur'an. Taha Husayn's book was reissued in a modified form in 1929.[44]

As soon as Pickthall returned to Hyderabad he published a review of some of the books he had bought in Cairo. In this review he referred sarcastically to

a certain scholar with a mania for the last Paris models in the way of thought [who] ... holds a high academic post, and his taste for foreign ideas includes half-baked or wholly unbaked theories concerning the Arabic language, history and Islam ... Of all the utterances of European Orientalists, this gleaner must needs pounce with rapture on the random shot of a facetious English professor renowned for his delight in throwing crackers at the Muslim world. And this particular squib is made the inspiration of the work withdrawn and now reissued after expurgation.[45]

And four years later he returned to the attack, accusing Taha Husayn (now named) as having demonstrably unsound premises and conclusions. Many people 'thought this especially deplorable since the author was in charge of Arabic studies at the new University'.[46]

Pickthall's translation has been in print since it was first published. Allen and Unwin obtained the licence from Knopf and published it in England in 1939. Pickthall worked on an edition that would satisfy some Muslims, with English on one page and the Arabic text opposite. He completed this within days of his final departure from India. With the support of the Nizam, a bilingual version was published in two volumes by the Government Press in Hyderabad. Allen and Unwin of London also took over this edition in 1976. In 1953 the English text was issued in New York as a paperback in the New American Library.

The translation itself has been translated. In 1958 the introduction and extracts were put into Turkish by Şinasi Siber and published in Ankara. Other extracts were translated by M. Şevki Alay and Ali Katiboğlu and published in Istanbul the same year.[47] In 1964 it was published in Portuguese in Mozambique and in 1970 a trilingual edition – English, Arabic and Urdu – appeared in Delhi. It has also appeared in Tagalog, the language of many Muslims in the Philippines.[48]

Pickthall conscientiously made himself familiar with European criticism, especially the work of Theodor Nöldeke and Josef Horovitz. But he is selective in what he accepts. He does not waver from an orthodox Muslim interpretation. He wrote an introduction to the work, giving an account of the circumstances of the revelation of the Qur'an, a precise and lucid yet comprehensive life of the Prophet. He also introduces each of the 114 *suras* or chapters, drawing attention to texts that reinforce his own Islamic views: the importance of conduct and the universality of Islam. In the text he avoids using the words 'Islam' or 'Muslims'. Earlier translations had used these words or else they had, as Pickthall put it, been 'left untranslated'. Pickthall thought this implied 'that they had at the time of revelation the technical meaning which they acquired afterwards'. He explained, 'I translate those words, as any Arab hearing them understands them, as "surrender" or "submission", "those who surrender" or "submit" (i.e. to Allah). For example the text which has always been translated "the religion with Allah is Islam" in my translation reads "religion with Allah consists in the surrender unto Him", which, besides being the accurate rendering, is a statement of a universal truth instead of a sectarian assertion.'[49]

The text with English on the left hand page and Arabic on the right was not published until after his death. This was the ideal presentation of a translation. It satisfied some conservative Muslim scruples and as such it became and remains a guide for Anglophone Muslims. The English can be seen to stand, not as a translation but as an explanation, a *tafsir* of the Arabic text. It has been accepted with least reserve by Muslims of India and Pakistan, as well as of Britain and the United States.

The authority of his Arabic has not gone unchallenged. In 1980 a successor of Pickthall as editor of *Islamic Culture*, Muhammad Asad, produced a new translation. He had not been satisfied with Pickthall's work feeling that 'his knowledge of Arabic was limited'.[50] And in the same year Professor Ahmed Ali in Pakistan announced that he planned a translation of the Qur'an because of inaccuracies in Pickthall's work.[51] President Zia ul-Haq had his attention drawn to alleged inaccuracies by Allama Syed Mohammed Razi Mujtahid in 1982. Pickthall was alleged to be 'not fully conversant with the Arabic language and idioms'.[52] The press report of this led to a furious letter in the Karachi newspaper, *Dawn*, from three of Pickthall's old Hyderabad students, Ghaziuddin Ahmed, Hameeduddin Ahmed and Mehdi Ali Siddiqi. They bore witness to 'the depth of his piety, his knowledge of the Qu'rân and his mastery of the Arabic language and Islamic learning'. The three angry gentlemen contemplated legal action, declaring that they were 'provoked into action because a translation so minutely scrutinized at Al-Azhar and generally accepted as correct all over the world for half a century is suddenly found to be "full of mistakes" by Allama Razi Mujtahid'.[53] They mobilized support and the Islamic Ideology Committee of Pakistan, under the chairmanship of the President of the Islamic Research Council, looked into the matter and found that Pickthall's translation was satisfactory. Some of the mistakes were due to misprints in the translation used. 'Others arose from Mujtahid's poor understanding of English.'[54]

Pickthall's final years were a serene anticlimax to his *jihad* years of the period from 1913 to 1930. During the early 1930s he suffered from malaria. He was never superbly fit nor did he spare himself physically.

He continued to have a talent for getting on famously with children. On one occasion he attended the wedding feast of a teacher in Hyderabad. As the senior guest, Pickthall found himself sitting next to the youngest guest, the six-year-old Anand Chandavarkar, who, half a century later remembers Pickthall

> immaculate in his European suit wearing a red fez cap but without the tassel, commonly worn by Muslims in Hyderabad ... He was the very embodiment of courtesy, a perfect synthesis of European and Oriental manners. We were seated together, lotus-position, on the carpeted floor before a lavish spread of the choicest Hyderabadi Moglai cuisine. He ate, like the rest of the assembly, with his

fingers, Indian-fashion without the slightest self-consciousness. As the dishes were being served, Pickthall, in fluent Urdu, albeit a little deliberate, turned to me. It was typical of him that he asked me whether I ate meat. He sensed that the answer would be no, as I was born and brought up a vegetarian till then, the child of Brahmin parents. Therefore he guided me, through the seemingly endless procession of delicacies, carefully pointing out the 'verboten' ones till the desserts, covered with silver foil, arrived. He asked me what books I liked (*Treasure Island* and *Grimm's Fairy Tales*) and what games I played. Cricket, of course! This delighted him no end and he was tickled when I proudly told him about my most cherished cricketer's autograph – that of the great Jack Hobbs on his only visit to India. . . . Sadly, I took leave of him.[55]

At the beginning of 1935, after ten years in the Nizam's service and before his sixtieth birthday, Pickthall retired. The Nizam presented him with a gold watch. Pickthall and his wife returned to England, meandering through Europe. He caught influenza and convalesced at the Savoie house of Mrs Huth Jackson in the South of France. They spent the winter of 1935–6 in Cornwall as far from the London cold as possible. In March 1936 he came up to London and addressed the Royal Central Asian Society on 'The Muslims in the Modern World' and returned to Cornish St Ives. He was contemplating a novel on the Spanish Islamic period and had many other plans – a revision of *The Cultural Side of Islam* and, above all, the performance of the pilgrimage to Mecca.

Pickthall was not afraid of death. In 1919 he had given a sermon on the *sura* from the Qur'an, *Ya Sin*, recited in the presence of the dying. Reflecting on death he said, 'I too shall go before that Judge today, tomorrow, in a few years' time. Only a little while remains to me at any rate, compared with all the precious moments I have spent already, and have wasted.'[56] One day in the middle of May he became unwell after lunch. The following morning after breakfast he rested, then got up and collapsed. He died at eleven o'clock on 19 May 1936 of coronary thrombosis.

The body was brought to the Muslim cemetery at Brookwood, Surrey, not far from Woking. It was lowered into the grave to funeral prayers delivered by the Imam of the Mosque on Saturday 23 May.

In India Pickthall had encouraged creative writing in English. In *Islamic Culture*, the Head of the Hyderabad City Improvement Board, Nizamat Jung, wrote a few classical lines of elegy to Muhammad Marmaduke Pickthall:

Soldier of faith! True servant of Islam!

To thee 'twas given to quit the shades of night
And onward move, aye onward into Light
With soul undaunted, heart assured and calm![57]

Part II

$$5.$$

THE NEAR EASTERN FICTION

'This ... is fiction, not fact; and, like all sound
fiction, is but truth in bloom.'

Pot au Feu

—— THE NEAR EASTERN SHORT STORIES ——

Tales of the Near East form the bulk of Pickthall's three volumes of short stories: *Pot au Feu* (1911), *Tales from Five Chimneys* (1915) and *As Others See Us* (1922). Twenty-eight stories have Near Eastern themes. Most are examples in miniature of Pickthall's ability to present the world from the point of view of the Near Easterner. All the stories take place in the generation or so before 1914 and most have the theme either of the social changes that affected Syria, Palestine, Egypt and Turkey during these years or of the role of foreigners and their relationships with the people of these lands.

Pickthall often sets the scene with a purple patch of description – the Mediterranean seen from the mountain villages of Syria or the reception room of a powerful chief. A character is introduced, and then a personal or moral dilemma is presented and resolved. Often misunderstandings arise from a clash of cultures. In 'The Battle of the Trees',[1] a line of telegraph poles is erected somewhere in Syria. Nearby villages remove them at night for use as building materials or firewood. Rival villages dispute claims on the analogy of a village's right to trees. Disputes lead to little local wars until the anonymous authorities bring in and set up telegraph poles made of hollowed

73

iron. 'A Case of Oppression'[2] tells of a poor old Egyptian who insists on occupying a workman's shed in the grounds of a house recently built. The new occupant of the house, an English judge, is puzzled, expects vacant possession and cannot understand the old man's obstinate presumption of right.

The tales include acute observations on European influences of speech and behaviour.

> Time was, within my memory, when children of the Mountain [Lebanon] mocked at Frankish trousers, shouting 'Hi, O my uncle, you have come in two!' But today all that is changed. Young native Christians wear cheap German slops to show their progress, they doff the fez when entering a house, an action formerly esteemed the greatest rudeness; they wear loud creaking boots, which are the mode out there, to advertise the difference from old-fashioned slippers, they decipher the Latin character more easily than the Arabic, and corrupt their mother-tongue with French and English.[3]

A Christian girl in Beirut 'wore her hair carried up to the top of her head in the mode of Europe, allowing a glimpse of the nape of her neck, which to every son of the East is ravishingly indecent'.[4] An Egyptian shaykh rises to grandeur 'owing to his natural talents and his readiness to trust new-fangled institutions such as banks and companies'.[5]

His Christians of Syria are culturally ambiguous. Throughout his stories Pickthall shows an animus against the Near Eastern Christians. They are portrayed as avaricious boozers, they comically ape the habits of the west. His animus influences Pickthall's moral view of murder as a social obligation. In 'The Marseilles Tragedy',[6] a young Greek Christian from Turkey kills his sister who has married a Muslim. It was her wish. The Muslim is tolerant and applies no pressure on her to adopt Islam. The brother gets grotesquely drunk and kills the sister he loves from a sense of family honour. Pickthall portrays it as an act of fanaticism. But in 'Melek',[7] the Turkish wife of a harmless old Turk calmly contemplates murdering her husband to advance the cause of the Turkish reformers. Pickthall presents this as a reluctant act of noble patriotism.

Hostility towards Christians is redeemed by one powerful story, 'An Ordeal by Fire',[8] which tells of the reactions of English people in a Turkish provincial town to a pogrom of Armenians. There is no sparing of feelings in the description of the massacre. 'The butchers went about their work methodically, much as the priests of old performed a sacrifice, beginning with 'Bismillah' and ending with the death-thrust. They killed a woman close to him with all this ritual, the officiators being three old men with long white beards, and anxious, kindly faces ... One of them stooped down and, ripping open the body of their victim, tore something out and beat it on the wall.'[9]

Pickthall's Europeans in the Near East are a mixed bunch. The missionaries are usually smug and aloof. Some Europeans try to understand. Most fail. Occasionally one becomes part of the local scenery such as 'an old French doctor, of long Oriental experience, who had adopted all the customs of the country saving abstinence'.[10] Others, new to the East, are fascinated. Dorothy Lee finds the talk of 'Count' Abdullah 'like the peepshow of an unknown world'.[11]

One of his most interesting characters is Sir Charles Duclay, KCMG, 'one of the rulers of Egypt and a famous Orientalist'.[12] Could he be based on Sir Ronald Storrs? Duclay is the narrator of an account of his friendship with a young Egyptian journalist, Abbas, who starts as a partisan of the British occupation. He supports the government and is disappointed when he does not receive support in return. He gets into trouble for criticizing the Khedive. The British do nothing to help him. Abbas becomes disillusioned and goes to England as a self-styled representative of the Egyptian nation. There he finds other similar representatives, longer established and better connected, who repudiate him. He returns to Egypt and gets involved in a terrorist organization and is arrested. Duclay goes to see him in prison. Abbas urges Duclay, for his soul's good, 'to leave the English and become a Muslim and an Oriental. It made me wince as if I had been stung.'[13] The reader is brought suddenly, almost ferociously, to the limits of Duclay's bland sympathies towards Abbas.

Pickthall is most original in describing the European, and usually the Englishman, through the eyes of the Arab, usually the Egyptian. Personal contact between Egyptians and Englishmen were rare, formal, restrained and usually for some official purpose, reminding both sides where power lay. An Englishman is described: 'The arbiter of life and death was tall and stiff and had a reddish beard. He wore spectacles, as they believed, on purpose to make his rigid face the more inscrutable.'[14] A clown at a fair caricatures the English official when 'he fished up a wig of tow which he adjusted to his head. He then rubbed some red dust upon his face until it wore the colour of pomegranate-bloom, put on a Frankish collar and an old pith helmet brought to him by an attendant, took in his hand a cane and began to strut up and down stiffly, with elbows raised, opening his mouth very wide and saying: "Wow! Wow!" at frequent intervals.' The Englishman eats 'meat and milk and vegetables, all duly stale from having been enclosed in tins for many years'.[15] His habits of recreation are incomprehensible. 'Armed with some curious sticks, he would take stand with legs apart and smite with all his strength a small white ball, pursuing it from place to place until he lost it.'[16] Onlooking village youngsters 'would mimic all unconsciously the strange grimaces which he made when bludgeoning the small white ball, which he seemed to look on as a sinful thing, his enemy'.[17]

One story, 'Karàkter'[18], is an eloquent commentary on the mystique of British rule in Egypt and an Egyptian's wish to share that mystique. A white-bearded old fellah petitions an English official. He wants karàkter to be acquired by his fourteen-year-old son, Ahmed, who is wearing a cheap gaudy ill-fitting European suit. 'Because I love my English lords,' the father explains, 'and admire their qualities, I would have my son instructed in Karàkter, by the knowledge of which they are above all else distinguished.'[19] The son has learnt some English by rote but is unable to use the language when the English official asks him an unexpected question. 'How should I know?' the boy mutters in Arabic. 'The Khawâjah is mad; he is cheating. It is not in the book.'[20] Ahmed however is sent to school in England. The years pass and Ahmed is a success at school. He goes on to Cambridge. His father then recalls him to Egypt. At first he is saddened but then he 'looked forward with a natural longing to his father's house, to the sight of camels raising dust upon the Nile-bank, of buffaloes wallowing and grunting in a reedy pool'.[21] His father is pleased: Ahmed now has character. The boast was no vain one. 'He had acquired the English character superficially just as he had learnt by heart whole text-books in old days at school. He could assume it instead of his own, at any minute. He could even constrain himself to think like an Englishman for hours at a stretch.'[22]

Through success in a public examination and his father's influence Ahmed gets an appointment as secretary to an English official in the Public Works Department. He and the Englishman get on tremendously just as Ahmed had got on with fellow students at Cambridge. But one day the Englishman is troubled about a trifle. Ahmed tries to help his friend:

'Don't be a fool, old man! Sit down. It's nothing, really.'
He [the Englishman] had been sitting back in his chair, with legs crossed nobly, in the English manner; next minute he was on his feet, his face livid, his body shaken from head to foot by shame and grief. For his friend he flashed round on him, ejaculating:
'Damn your insolence! What the hell do you mean by speaking to me like that?'
The clerk of lower grade was grinning from ear to ear.

'Why, whateffer did I say?' questioned Ahmed, his voice trembling with rage.

A flood of oaths was the answer. Ahmed drew himself up.

'I haf you know, sir, I haf been to Cambridge.'

'Go to hell!'

And when the clerk had retired, the still angry Englishman quoted, as he sat down again at his desk, a vile Arabic proverb, an invention of the Turks, to the effect that if you encourage Ali, he will presently defile your carpet. It was an offence unthinkable.[23]

The Englishman tries to make amends, but in vain. The mystique of Karàkter is exploded and Ahmed, to cut a short story shorter, becomes a nationalist. The story is totally credible, enlivened by the English of Ahmed, the fluently colloquial switching, under stress, to inadequate control of English consonants. His diction is wounded with his pride.

'Karàkter' and other stories placed in Egypt are authentic records in fictional form. He describes the extent of Egyptian endorsement, even enthusiasm for British rule, an acceptance of British claims for their authority and the wide range of personal relationships – friendly, correct, respectful, hurt, formal, uncomprehending – that linked British and Egyptian. Such a range is impossible to record with precision in works of history or sociology. Like a photographer Pickthall has taken snapshots of psychological history, elusive scenes that have been forgotten or ignored by Englishman and Egyptian alike.

———SAÏD THE FISHERMAN (1903)———

Saïd the Fisherman is Pickthall's best-known novel and deservedly so. It is less hastily composed than later Near Eastern novels. The experiences of his two years' travel are transmuted into a splendid yarn. It shows up for the first time Pickthall's powers of sustained observation. Popular tales, turns of phrase, physical habits and gestures, the social and political conditions of late nineteenth-century Syria are meticulously and accurately described.

The book took a long time to write. Pickthall supplemented his own memories with background derived from books written by James H. Skene who was British Consul in Aleppo in 1860 and by C.H. Churchill who wrote from personal experience of the Druze of Lebanon in the 1850s and 1860s. He also met Mrs Skene in Switzerland in early 1899 and discussed the events of 1860 with her.

Saïd the Fisherman received immediate critical acclaim. At first sales were slow. Only eight hundred copies were sold in the first two months but by 1904 it had reached a fifth edition, by 1913 a cheap ninth edition and in 1927 a fourteenth edition. It was published in 1903 in the United States, republished by Knopf in 1923 and issued in the Blue Jade Library in 1925. It has been translated into German and Italian. Oriental scholars like Edward Browne, Stanley Lane-Poole and D.S. Margoliouth saw it as a masterpiece. Lord Cromer became a fan. H.G. Wells, Arnold Bennett and James Barrie were enthusiastic when it was published and as late as 1928 D.H. Lawrence wrote a warm article on the book in *Adelphi.*

Saïd, the central character of the novel, is by profession a fisherman, by nature a scamp. When we first meet him he is about twenty-three years of age, has been married to Hasneh for seven years, is childless and practises his trade on the Palestine coast near Haifa. He gives up fishing and sets off for Damascus, abandoning his wife on the way. To all whom he meets he lies and poses in order to defraud and to escape disaster. He reaches Damascus and there lives a hand-to-mouth existence.

He arrives in Damascus in the summer of 1860. In the previous months there have been rumours of strife and a build-up of tension between the Christian community on the one side and the Muslims and Druze on the other. Saïd's acquaintances in the city are humble Muslim folk but we get direct and indirect glimpses of the great. The noble *amir* Abdul Qadir, the exiled Algerian, makes honourable appearances. Saïd's closest companion, Selim, is for a while a servant in the household of the vacillating *wali* of Damascus, Ahmad Pasha. Saïd is, with other young Muslims, arrested and obliged to sweep the streets of the Christian quarter – a humiliating punishment that leads to riots and to the massacre of hundreds of Christians.[24] During these riots Saïd abducts the young daughter of a Christian merchant after whom he has long lusted and sets himself up as a carpet seller.

In the years after 1860 Saïd prospers. He marries his Christian captive, Ferideh, and has a son. But his self-confidence leads him to overreach himself. He is betrayed and robbed by Ferideh. He loses his friends, becomes an outcast and tries to escape from Syria. In Beirut he eludes pursuit by the police and swims to a boat bound for England. He disembarks in east London, penniless and friendless. He becomes crazed and a Christian missionary rescues him and arranges for him to be taken to Egypt. In Alexandria he escapes from his rescuers and is succoured as a holy madman until 1882 when, intoxicated by the riots against the Christians, he meets his death imagining he is upholding the honour of the religion of the Prophet.

Saïd is an amoral rogue, a hypocrite, capable of extremes of cruelty and callousness. He is vain, covetous, deceitful, faithless and engaging. There is a Falstaffian irrepressibility about him. We are seduced into accepting behaviour and attitudes that are morally unacceptable. Saïd is most outrageous when he is poor. Prosperity permits him to pose as a pious Damascus notable and makes him less interesting. In Saïd, Pickthall has created an unforgettable personality.

Having accepted Saïd, we are drawn to see the world and the west from Saïd's perspective. On his way to Damascus he breaks into the house of a western missionary. He wanders into the bedroom and marvels at the central article of furniture that 'was almost like a table standing on six iron legs; but four of the legs reached above as well as below, and each of the four was crowned with a little knob, like an orange of some burnished yellow metal he took for gold. A wonderful thing!'[25]

In the London chapters we see London as Saïd does. He tries to make sense of a hostile environment and reacts to human situations as if he were still in Damascus – standing on his dignity, fearful lest he taste forbidden flesh, seizing opportunities to pray, cursing Christians. Not for a moment does the narrative flag. Not once is there an ironic aside that would display the values of the author or appeal to those of the reader. We suffer as Saïd suffers – from mudslinging ragamuffins, officious policemen and harassed womenfolk.

Most of the book takes place in Damascus. We meet a host of Damascenes. Saïd's best friend, Selim, acts as his conscience. 'Selim was a good Muslim, a man pious and devout both at practice and at heart. Had he been born to wealth and eminence he would have been revered of all men for a saint.'[26] Whenever Saïd disregards Selim's advice – which he does repeatedly – disaster follows.

In his description of people and relationships there is a total absence of moralizing or of sentimentality. Relationships are based on inequality; a balance of deference and patronage. Saïd behaves normally when, in the days of his prosperity, many greet him respectfully in the street, and he acknowledges their presence 'by the slightest scooping of his hand. But a notable of the city, riding by on a grey horse, heralded by an outrider, with cries of "Oäh!" scattering the crowd to right and left, Saïd was foremost of all to bow his head and touch his lips and brow in token of reverence.'[27] There is a careful and precise hierarchy, universally though tacitly recognized.

Pickthall describes the atmosphere leading up to the riots of 1860. The narrative of Saïd's struggle for survival is broken by rumour and statements of Muslim resentment of the new privileges granted to Christians under the pressure from Western powers. A muleteer complains that Christians have grown fat and insolent. 'The fault,' he says, 'is with the consuls, who shield and abet them in whatever they do. The worst of them will tell you that they are French subjects or Muscovite, and will show papers to that effect given to them by the Consul.'[28] The Muslims feel helpless for 'the Franks are powerful and their vengeance would be dire. As thou knowest, the French and English gave aid to the Turks in the late Muscovite war, and in return they claim to govern the Sultan's realm instead of him.'[29]

Idealized descriptive passages are invaded by a brutal almost obscene realism. Sound and sights combine to produce a pretty tableau of a village on the outskirts of Damascus.

> At the foot of the hill, on the utmost fringe of the gardens, he could see a little village of flat-topped houses. A string of camels was drawing near to it along the base of the steep. The twinkle of their bells rippled in the twilight cheerily. Of a sudden the noise of chanting arose – a wild, delicious song of piercing shrillness. It came from the high platform of the only minaret of the village. Somewhat mellowed by the distance, it reached Saïd's ears as heavenly music. The clangour of bells ceased of a sudden. The camels had halted. Their drivers, obedient to the muezzin's call, were prostrate in prayer.[30]

But a little later, as Saïd rode (on a stolen horse) into the city, 'dogs, seemingly without number, rose grudgingly and slunk snarling from the roadway.'[31]

Menacing hounds repeatedly hover, reminding us constantly not to be swept away by pretty pictures. In the opening pages of the book a description of a glorious sunset on the Palestine coast takes in a pack of dogs who 'were lying replete about the body of a dead donkey at the edge of the ripples, panting drowsily with their tongues out. They blinked at him as he passed and their bellies heaved uneasily. They were too full to snarl.'[32] In the city dogs come into their own at night. Dogs in Damascus 'prowled watchful on the skirts of the crowd, aware that man's intrusion was almost over, looking forward with dripping jaws to an undisturbed feast of refuse'.[33] By contrast, during the day, 'the street dogs prowled with lolling tongues as they slept'.[34] It is fitting that when the Muslim mob want to insult the Christians, at Saïd's instigation 'they took hold of the street-dogs which lay around them by dozens, tied a cross under the tail of each, and with a kick sent them howling in all directions'.[35]

The novel gives a plausible picture of tenuous provincial Ottoman rule. Its authority was limited by local circumstances and was capricious in nature. Bribery favoured the well-to-do. But for most people the government was 'remote as the sky, something impassive, neither friend nor foe. He had stood in the same vague awe of it that a simple man has of some mighty engine whose working is a mystery to him.'[36] The book is a descriptive secondary source for the state of nineteenth-century Ottoman Syria, based on the oral traditions Pickthall himself gathered during his youthful travels.

Pickthall wrote as he saw the Near East. He often asserted that he had fallen in love with Islam and 'the orient' during the 1890s. *Saïd the Fisherman* was read by many who did not share Pickthall's love. And they found reasons for hostility or contempt for Syrians and Muslims. Saïd's personality dominates the book. A common western criticism of Islam was the combination of formal dignity with sensuality and vulgarity.[37] During the Damascus riots there was a lull. 'The unbelievers enjoyed a respite while the faithful said their prayers.' Amidst the slaughter, Saïd himself 'fell on his face and gave praise and thanks to Allah. It pleased him to think on how few days of his life he had omitted to pray at each appointed hour.'[38] It is as if Pickthall is giving fuel to Islam's critics. Yet this conclusion is misleading. Virtue is often boring. There are good Muslims in *Saïd the Fisherman*. Selim, Saïd's conscience, is a paragon of virtue. The novel also contains Pickthall's first example of a recurrent type of character – the civilized and gentle Muslim aristocrat, kind yet stern, understanding human fraility but not straying from the path of virtue, good conduct and example, a man who, in short, followed the precepts Pickthall spoke and wrote about in his later Islamic years.

———THE HOUSE OF ISLAM (1906) ———

The House of Islam is disappointing. Pickthall's second Near Eastern novel lacks the intensity and measured preparation of *Saïd the Fisherman*.

The story is mostly set in nineteenth-century Jerusalem. It displays the contrast in Islamic life-styles of two brothers, Milhem and Shems-ud-din. Both are of Palestinian origin. The novel opens in Constantinople. Milhem is an ambitious Ottoman official. His brother is a merchant and a holy man. Milhem borrows money from Shems-ud-din to purchase a government post in Jerusalem. Shems-ud-din withdraws to private life in Transjordan, to a town with classical ruins and a community of Circassians who have been settled there after the Crimean War.

Shems-ud-din has a much loved daughter, Alia, who falls ill. He is persuaded to take her to a Frankish doctor in Jerusalem. He has acquired a reputation for piety and orthodoxy and sets off for Jerusalem in the company of Hassan, the Circassian leader of a band of bandits, who had been present at the siege of Kars. The adventures are picaresque, tedious and unconvincing. Saïd's adventures in Damascus may have been equally improbable but Saïd was a rounded villian and the circumstances of his life were composed of such authentic detail that made the improbabilities credible. Not so *The House of Islam*.

Pickthall is presenting dilemmas facing the Muslims and alternate ways of resolving these dilemmas. There are, for example, three ways of coping with illness. You can trust in God. This is Shems-ud-din's initial response. But friends advise recourse to the benefits of western infidel medical practice. Hassan recalls an English doctor, the memory of whose honourable behaviour at Kars offset the English betrayal of the Circassians after the Crimean War. A third is that preferred by Alia's maid who recommends the curative properties of a tree at the tomb of a local saint. Secretly she attaches some of Alia's clothes to the tree. Shems-ud-din condemns this local heresy and is shocked when he sees his daughter's clothes on the tree. But his rejection is mixed with unease. 'In tearing down the idolatrous rag from off the branch, he had accepted his daughter's death at the hand of the Lord.'[39]

Jerusalem is described with the same verve as Damascus in *Saïd the Fisherman*. It is the city of sophisticated, supercilious and busy townsmen.

> To any one threading that crowded labyrinth of whitish stone, ancient and coherent, glimpses of the pure blue sky became welcome as a flower on rocks. For Shems-ud-din, accustomed through so many years to wide horizons and an open road, the overshadowing walls made a prison. The hubbub of the bazaars dazed him, and he felt hurt by the careless shouldering of other wayfarers.[40]

The Muslim quarter is described with the sensitivity of one who has been there.

> Old walls rose high on either hand. Jutting lattices, with here and there an arch, enroached on the jewel sky. In the shade of the ancient portal, ornate but crumbling to decay, sat a breadseller asleep behind two tiers of flat brown loaves. A man with a water-skin on his back turned in at the doorway of a house before them. A grave notable, in apparel sober but rich, passed them without a glance, one hand in his breast. Everything in that dim, once splendid quarter told of a proud reserve, of a dignity that needs no trump for its assertion. The air was sad with the sadness of great things past.[41]

The romantic picture of Jerusalem is as usual not sentimentalized. We also have a love song, sung to the accompaniment of a lute. Now the song 'rose to a frenzied howl, now sank to a passionate moan. From time to time, among the hiddenways beneath, a strife of dogs broke out, raged noisily for a space, and then subsided.'[42]

Many of the minor themes

Many of the minor themes of *Saïd the Fisherman* appear but without the coherence of the earlier work. The Europeans are neither named nor individualized but are just as comic. 'The Franks made a great clatter with knives and forks upon plates of tin or some other metal. They laughed loud and vacantly, rousing echoes among the cliffs. They stared rudely at the newcomers.'[43] They are seen from the Arab perspective. From such a point of view many of their domestic habits are odd: such as sitting on chairs. Shems-ud-din is obliged to sit on one, 'his feet tucked under him as far as the awkwardness of the contrivance would allow'.[44]

But these moments of insight are few in number. It was as if *Saïd the Fisherman* had used up Pickthall's reserves of memories. This second eastern tale is using fragments of the experiences and traditions garnered ten years earlier. In his next novel, *The Myopes*, one of the central characters writes on his eastern experiences. An editor rejects his writings with criticisms that apply to *The House of Islam*. The writer is 'part of the show unconsciously ... and can't get out of it to have a look. In fact, his critical faculty is almost entirely undeveloped.'[45] *The House of Islam* is a curiously tired book. It was published just before his journey to Egypt where he was able to recapture the inspiration of transforming the ordinary incidents of life into works of art.

—— *THE CHILDREN OF THE NILE* (1908) ——

The Children of the Nile was the fruit of Pickthall's visit to Egypt in 1907. It was a contribution to the debate on the events of Britain's involvement in Egypt a quarter of a century earlier. The debate was prompted by Cromer's retirement as Consul General in Cairo in 1907 and the publication of his Egyptian memoirs, *Modern Egypt*, in 1908. The case against Britain's involvement was made by Wilfrid Scawen Blunt in *Secret History of the English Occupation of Egypt* published in 1907. Pickthall's novel also records with great acuteness some of the social changes undergone in Egypt in the nineteenth century.

The novel relates events in Cairo, Alexandria and the Nile delta in the years leading up to the battle of Tel-el-Kebir, September 1882, when Wolseley's British army smashed the nationalist uprising led by 'Arabi Pasha. The central character of the novel is Mabrûk, the son of a Delta shaykh, who receives a European education in the School of Medicine in Cairo and reads soppy romances in Arabic translated from English or French. Mabrûk is seen in three settings. The first is the life of the village of his childhood, with its feuds and dealings with brigands. Brigandage flourished in the 1870s and 1880s and Pickthall observes the positive social role of brigands. Secondly several chapters describe the fair at Tanta, commemorating Sayyid Ahmad Badawi, the most beloved of popular Egyptian saints. Thirdly, Mabrûk joins 'Arabi's army and is caught up as a close observer of the events of 1882: the riots and bombardment of Alexandria and the battle of Tel-el-Kebir itself.

Pickthall, like other historical novelists, avoids making authentic major historical personalities the central characters of his fiction. We see the great men of history from the wings. Mabrûk takes a message to 'Arabi. 'The famous peasant soldier', is described as 'a tall, thick-set man, deliberate and something ponderous, but urbane, and owner of a very pleasant smile.'[46] Pickthall analyses the support 'Arabi's revolt has. Peasants and villagers, the lower ranks of the army, formed the backbone of his movement. The merchants of the cities who flourished in quiet times held back. Many of the privileged classes, Turks and Circassians, gave him support out of opportunism though they retained a measure of detachment.

The world is seen through Mabrûk's eyes and social changes are described as they affect him. Printing developed enormously in Egypt during the century. There were manuals for doing things and also a literature of imagination. The literate had their intellectual and creative horizons expanded and extended as never before. Mabrûk is a dreamer, a player of roles. The expanded horizons had an effect on people's expectations and aspirations. Mabrûk 'saw the process by which ills which had hitherto been regarded as natural, and from the hand of Allah, were elevated into grievances and laid at the door of the Government'.[47] But to transform the politics of Egypt and to mobilize people into collective constructive action was not easy. 'For action, it was necessary either to convince each individual that he personally stood to gain by a change of government, or else to furnish a display of power so formidable as to set the whole world cringing.'[48]

The novel shows up popular attitudes that were cynical and opportunistic, brutal and selfishly immoral. Mabrûk's father could have bought Mabrûk out of the army, but such conspicuous consumption would have attracted brigands, robbers and tax collectors: 'it would have advertised his wealth and led to ruin.'[49] When Mabrûk became a junior officer it 'warmed his heart to order men about like dogs, and beat the stupid ones with his cane. He himself had been ordered about and caned – a fact which gave his present work a taste of justice.'[50] The attitudes are those of folk with a background of living on the margin of subsistence, people who had to live by their wits in an uncertain capricious world. Faith was one thing but survival was another. Burckhardt's collection of Egyptian proverbs a century earlier shows the same rough and humourous cynicism.

The Delta's world of faith, routine and submission was being changed by a host of influences from outside. Alternative patterns of life expressed themselves in tangible and physical ways. Egyptian Cairo has vitality but is encroached upon by modernity.

> Leaving behind the spacious streets of the modern quarter, they threaded a maze of alleys teeming with careless life, where full dogs slept by the foot of the walls, and every doorway breathed forth homely smells. Some of the conscripts had begun to weep anew, when they emerged upon a vast meydân, surrounded by great dull buildings on a foreign pattern. Here a band was playing, while soldiers moved about coherently, fifties and hundreds of them appearing in their evolutions only as slabs and slices from a general mass.[51]

Routine becomes regimentation; careless life gives way to drill.

Mabrûk and his wife accept and embrace the foreign influences. Dress was frequently the indicator of their acceptance. When Mabrûk enters a train dressed in a Frankish suit, the Muslim passengers at first assume that he is a Christian. 'The fashion of a Frankish suit beneath the fez,' observed Pickthall, 'though growing frequent in the town among young Muslims of advanced ideas, in the provinces was still restricted to rich Copts and Syrians.'[52] His wife found the village women rude. They 'were always mocking her refinement and the notions she had brought back from the town. To be unveiled in the sight of men had shocked her modesty at first returning.' (The wearing of the veil, in the 1880s as in the 1980s, was a symbol of upwardly mobile urban women.) 'She missed the din, the tempting shops, the merry sights, the romps with the other women at the baths.'[53] But, though assumed, these urban traits of behaviour were recognized as superficial, even despised. Such behaviour was 'an apish trick or antic of the brain, only valuable as giving him among his present associates a vogue like that of the juggler or skilled story-teller'.[54]

As in the other novels, the Englishman is a gawky outsider. The soldiers at Tel-el-Kebir have 'broad red faces with pale vacant eyes and spreading noses'.[55] But there is a difference. Politically Pickthall is no friend of the Nationalist hostility towards British rule. He saw merit in the European influence and the British occupation. Soldiers and public servants were regularly paid. The English were personally popular. 'Loud were the praises of their generosity. The English manners, English speech, were in the air. Young men of fashion who used to say, "Banjû" in the French way, now said "Good-ah-day" at sight of one another.'[56] Even Mabrûk's time-serving father is enthusiastic for the 'good Inklîz, who, it is well seen, are the lords of generosity!'[57]

In Syria Pickthall had been introduced to the country through missionaries. He reacted against them and preferred the company of Syrians. In Egypt Pickthall was the guest of British officials. He does not repudiate the official viewpoint as his journalism indicates. *The Children of the Nile* is the first of his novels in which there is an implicit political commitment. His insights into popular attitudes are as shrewd as those of *Saïd the Fisherman*. And, as in the earlier novel, he does not flatter. But there is also a love, an enjoyment of the exuberance of the popular festivals, a sensitivity to subtle shifts in behaviour. Such sympathy was not the sympathy of Blunt who wholeheartedly espoused first the Arabist and later the Nationalist cause. Pickthall would have sympathized with one of his characters in *The Children of the Nile*, a young man of noble background and great wealth, with property in Damasus. 'In truth, he belonged to no one province, but to El Islâmîyeh, and was as much at home in Samarkand or Mekka as here in Egypt. Viewing this world from the heights of true religion, he saw its political concerns, for the most part, as only a strife of base ambitions, of which the strivers would be ashamed at the Last Day.'[58] Commitment to the world of Islam and detachment from strife for advancement or temporal gain becomes a common theme in Pickthall's later Islamic thinking. The quiet people preserved the faith. It did not greatly matter in whose hands rested the reigns of power – so long as justice prevailed and religion flourished. Such ends were achieved when Egypt was controlled by red-faced loud-speaking Englishmen. His Egyptian novel did not upset Pickthall's English hosts in Cairo.

——— THE VALLEY OF THE KINGS (1909) ———

The Valley of the Kings is a tale of guile and gullibility. Its setting is a coastal town of Palestine round the time of Pickthall's early wanderings there. The central character is a poor Palestinian Christian called Iskender from an Orthodox family who has been educated at an English mission school. The senior nun is called Carûlîn. (One of Pickthall's step-sisters, called Caroline, became briefly an Anglican nun in South Africa.) Iskender has a talent for painting and has disgraced himself by misinterpreting encouragement from one of the younger nuns and making a pass at her. On the rebound he becomes besotted by a travelling young Englishman whose name we never know but whose standing is inflated by Iskender and the town's dragomans to that of a prince, an emîr. We see him as Iskender sees him, and it is only as the Emîr that he is referred to throughout the book. Iskender and the Emîr wander off to the Valley of the Kings, presumably Petra, in search of gold that Iskender has dreamt of. Illness and disillusion follow and the Emîr bitterly and contemptuously throws Iskender over.

The novel is simply told and there is constant tension between the tug of Iskender's roots and his dreams and aspirations. His roots are represented by the Orthodox community with, at its local head, the wily grasping sagacious old priest Mitri who has both a beautiful daughter and some of the best lines of the book. Mitri, personifying the community, appreciates the need to coexist with others. He is critical of the proselytizing of the missionaries. 'They suppose that what is good for their race must be good for all the others, thus ignoring the providence of Allah, who made the peoples of the earth to differ in appearance, speech, and manners.'[59] Like the Christians of Constantinople before the Ottoman conquest of 1453, he prefers the turban to the Pope. 'With the Muslims we have in common language, country, and the intercourse of daily life. Therefore, I say, a Muslim is less abominable before Allah than a Latin or a Brôtestânt.'[60]

Iskender's loyalties are torn between the Anglican mission and the Orthodox community. The field for the conflict is Iskender's consuming passion – painting. He is encouraged and patronized by one of the sisters and then by the Emîr who has a paint box sent out from England. Iskenders's instinct is to make the most important object he represents occupy the largest portion of his canvas. He paints a scene of bedouins and is impressed by the camel. He drew it so big 'that it bestrode the whole page of his drawing-book; while the camp itself, the sandhills, some scattered houses and a palm-tree in the distance, the very sky, seemed no more than the pattern of a carpet upon which it stood'.[61] Here Pickthall, another of whose step-sisters was an art student, is describing the traditions of Byzantine art, the tradition of Orthodox icon painting. Both the younger sister at the mission and the Emîr try to advise Iskender on perspective. But his Orthodox patrons care not for such realism. 'That the Franks have a pretty, life-like trick is undeniable,' says one, 'yet I think our ancient style, stiff and conventional as they call it, is far more reverent.'[62]

Iskender is torn. 'He belonged to nobody.'[63] In the first anguished two thirds of the book he desperately wants to be liked by the Englishman. This wish to be loved leads him to deceive the Emîr and to get both into scrapes. The priest, Mitri, tells him:

> 'Now thy dream was to be a Frank in all save birth, to associate with thy Emîr on equal terms. To that end all thy follies were invented. The wish was foolish only. But to put it into practice, that was fatal to thee – a crime in all men's eyes . . . Allah made thee a son of the Arabs. Accept the part allotted, and give up aping that which thou canst never be.'[64]

The last third of the book sees Iskender accepting his identity, returning to the Orthodox fold, marrying the priest's daughter, being apprenticed to a famous painter of icons in Jerusalem, and purging his style 'of just those lifelike touches which these fools admire'[65] and settling happily into the community of his fathers. 'For the first time in his life he felt at home in his own land. The whole of the Orthodox community were henceforth his brethren.'[66] When Protestant Arabs remonstrate with him for his apostacy he invariably replies, 'I am a son of the Arabs . . . and have no wish to seem to be a Frank.'[67] The novel ends with an exuberant procession round the Orthodox church, bearing a new and magnificent icon of St George painted by Iskender. An old rival appears, a Protestant Arab, recently returned from England and with an English wife. 'In a flash he remembered things he had forgotten, recalled a standpoint that had once seemed all desirable. He perceived how ludicrous this joyful marching round must seem to English eyes.'[68] The doubts appear, flicker and are extinguished at once.

Once again Pickthall registers minutiae of changing social and sartorical habits in Palestine. Iskender's uncle and mother set out for a walk. She gathers up her skirt with one hand and places the other on the arm of her brother-in-law, 'ready crooked to receive it. "It is the fashionable way," she titters as they set forth.'[69] His mother, a charlady at the mission, has remained loyal to the Protestant community and reminds Iskender's wife of what has been forgone. 'Thou wouldst wear fine Frankish clothes of wondrous textures, and hats, I tell thee, hats with waving feathers.'[70]

The novel also records impressions of pre-1914 Palestine. It records an Arab consciousness felt particularly among the Orthodox community. The priest, Mitri, reflects that advancement in his church is closed to him 'since all the chief among the monks are foreign Greeks who despise us sons of the Arab and would keep us down'.[71] Iskender in opting for his Arab identity prefers 'the insolent domination of the Muslim, his blood-relative, to the arrogance of so-called Christian strangers'.[72]

The Valley of the Kings was one of the more successful of Pickthall's novels. J.M. Dent reprinted it for their series The Wayfarers' Library, in 1914. It anticipates *Oriental Encounters* in its affectionate account of a Palestine that was fast fading. It is of particular historical significance in its awareness of embryonic Arab nationalism, or at least an Arab consciousness that transcended the confessional abyss.

———————— VEILED WOMEN (1913) ————————

Veiled Women is perhaps Pickthall's most ambitious novel. In it he is explaining, describing and justifying harim life. It is the story of an English orphan, Mary Smith, who goes to Cairo in the 1860s to be the governess of the prosperous Turco-Egyptian family of Muhammad Pasha Salih. She and the Pasha's son, Yusuf, fall in love. She becomes a Muslim and they marry. Two of their children survive infancy. One child, Muhammad, is killed shortly before the battle of Tel-el-Kebir in 1882.

The narrative concentrates on two periods: the year or so of the betrothal and early years of marriage, and the period of the 'Arabi revolt, 1879–82. Although Mary is the principal character she is seen and described from the standpoint of the women of the household. Indeed we learn her English name almost incidentally one third of the way through the book. Throughout she is called Barakah.

The course of the marriage is not smooth. Barakah suffers from boredom. She is told that she is free to move but only within harim restraints. She goes off one day for a walk to nearby villages, and although she is fittingly and modestly dressed, this initiative creates a scandal. She is jostled in the village by men who cannot accept that a well-dressed woman should thus walk the streets. Her behaviour causes consternation to her adoptive family. Her father-in-law, the Pasha, cannot understand walking abroad for pleasure. 'You assure me that you walked for pleasure,' he incredulously says, 'I could understand it in a garden, round and round. But when it is a case of going anywhere – Grand Dieu!'[73] The rest of the household attribute the walk to a love affair with an Englishman, to sunstroke, to madness or – the most popular explanation – to possession by a malignant spirit.

Barakah has embraced harim life with tact and enthusiasm, but goes through periods of ennui when she finds it all irksome. 'The food, too highly spiced, did not agree with her; the sanitary arrangements were disgusting; she noticed failings not observed before, particularly in the behaviour of the servants to her.'[74] When she falls ill she suffers the officious – though loving and caring – attentions of the womenfolk. 'Illness, like death and birth, was woman's great occasion, when, guarding the traditions, she stood forth as a priestess.'[75]

The benign Pasha pays for Yusuf and Barakah to go for a break to Paris. They go in a party with other young friends. The Paris holiday becomes a farce. The women are left in the hotel while the men go off on their own. By each of the men, including her husband, Barakah is asked how they can win the hearts of the presumably available French women. After a grotesque and humiliating public brawl Yusuf accedes to Barakah's suggestion that they go to Switzerland for a few days. 'She longed to walk by forest streams, beneath great mountains, in solitude, with keen, cool breezes to restore her spirits.'[76] But the visit, satisfying to Barakah, is not a success. The mountains terrify Yusuf. When they approach Egypt, the thought of the Nile is pleasing. 'Thy Nile,' he says, 'is smooth and good to drink, not putrid and forever kicking like the sea.'[77]

Barakah in time resigns herself to her fate as an Egyptian housewife. There are other moments of anguish and distress. Her son, Muhammad, turns out to be a bully, proud of his Turkish blood, selfish and contemptuous of others. Barakah indulges him to the scandal of the harim who nag the head of the house, old Muhammad Pasha Salih, to remove his grandson from Barakah's care, and have him brought up by a sterner female relation. When cornered and obliged to recognize the path of disagreeable duty, the Pasha, 'fingering his beads, observed that God is merciful'.[78] He remarks to his son 'that when women take that tone – "of thy great kindness, deign to listen", and the rest, there is no safe course for man but to obey.'[79]

The central theme of the novel is the pace of life in the harim. Barakah found that the world of women was

> a great republic, with liberties extending to the meanest slave, and something of the strength that comes of solidarity. Unless in jealous fury, no woman would inform against another, bond or free; nor fail to help her in the hour of need. They had their shibboleths, their customs, their rites and ceremonies, even their courts of justice, independent of the world of men. Each lady owning slaves controlled them absolutely. Her husband never saw their faces, hardly knew them. The law against his making love among them, except by her command, was very drastic. The child

of such a union would have been her slave. If he required a concubine, he had to buy, not steal one. So sacred with the Muslims was the married woman's right to property – a right which was not recognized at all in England.[80]

The life of the harim was often given over to the tedious sybaritism of harmless indulgences: gossip, sweetstuffs, cigarettes and the nargileh. But there is also a dark side. 'Many an enlightened Muslim would have died of horror had he known the works of darkness countenanced by his harîm – the sacrifices to malignant beings; the veneration paid to hoary negresses for demonaical possession; the use to which the name of God was sometimes put.'[81] And there are several references to the *zar*, an exclusively female ritual which either exorcises or appeases the spirits believed to possess an ailing body. When Barakah was seriously ill after the birth of a son, the orthodox attentions of an Italian doctor seemed to be in vain. The women then hung garlic in her room, 'burnt potent odours till the air grew suffocating, and dosed the patient with a paste compounded of the dust of mummies mixed with human milk.'[82] This was no more successful than the ministrations of European medicine. So the women bring in a kid and several live fowls and take over Barakah's sickroom for two hours one afternoon, to hold a zar.

Many servants, female children, and familiars of the household trooped in with noiseless feet and squatted down along the wall. Then came a group of half a dozen negresses, fantastically dressed in rags of finery, with ringing anklets; one of whom embraced a struggling little goat, while others bore live chickens by the feet. Bold-eyed and with a swaggering gait, they marched up to the bed, and seemed to offer up the fowls and kid to Barakah, who could not understand the words they uttered in a screeching chant. Then they danced back to an adjoining room, of which the door stood open. Upon the threshold madness seemed to seize them. They fell upon the kid with cries of glee. The creature, bleeding piteously, was flung into an earthen bowl placed there in readiness. Amid mad laughter knives were brandished and brought down, hands helped to extract the creature's life. The fowls were likewise gashed and torn asunder; the matting round grew foul with steaming entrails. Another minute and the slayers reappeared, their black arms purpled to the elbow, dripping blood, their faces and their lips defiled with it; and then began a devilish dance of self-abandonment, all the more horrible for its approach to beauty. The sleek skin of the dancers caught the blue lights; their fixed eyes gleamed enormous, like those painted on the lids of mummies.

Barakah believed herself in hell, for ever lost; it was as if an iron hand compressed her throat. Her heart beat wildly. One of the women, the most shameless, lurched towards her, stretching out a blod-stained hand. Her heart gave one tremendous beat and then stood still.[83]

Strange to say, she recovered.

Pickthall notes that the zar, in the 1860s, was 'the latest novelty'.[84] This is an interesting observation, based presumably on the findings of his own wanderings in Egypt in 1907, the year in which he sets the last chapter of *Veiled Women*. In this, an aging Barakah reflects with her friends on the changes in her life. She accepts Islam and an unequal role for women. She is nostalgic for old values but recognizes that surface changes do not affect the essential.

Once again Pickthall is an acute observer of subtle changes in habits: the emancipated Egyptian woman speaks French but slips off to see the old crone who prescribes some ghastly remedy for a tiresome ailment; apprehension about European-inspired innovations 'in which the hand of unbelief was plainly visible';[85] the advent of a new Islamic century, AH 1300, when a new prophet might be expected; the identification of the Islamic deliverer with 'a simple soldier, who ventured to oppose the wicked rulers';[86] the lofty social contempt of the Turkish ruling class towards 'Arabi Pasha. Pickthall uses fiction to capture attitudes, feelings, types. He portrays three generations of the Turco-Egyptian family, each of them three dimensional, credible characters, rooted in their society. Barakah's father-in-law, the kindly Pasha, whose family rose to prominence with Muhammad 'Ali early in the century, is ever courteous, kindly and anxious to understand. His son, Barakah's husband, is a bore. He is middle-aged at the time of the 'Arabi revolt. He joins in reluctantly but, after 'Arabi's defeat, he less reluctantly becomes a Minister under the British occupation.

> He had attained the wisdom which comes easily to middle age, hated disturbance and distrusted novelty . . . Politics had been for him a well-ruled game, on which a man would be a fool to waste vitality. As a functionary, he had lounged on sofas, telling beads, dictating orders to his secretary, at ease except when called before superiors.[87]

His son is an enthusiast for the 'Arabi revolt, enthusiastic not for a fellah revolution but against an infidel occupation of Egypt. His Turkish pride (absent in his more Turkish grandfather) is cruel and vicious. He joins 'Arabi's army as a fifteen-year-old lad. Family influence enables him to be a training officer in charge of new recruits, village lads and men. He is impatient with them, insults them, beats them. 'I beat and beat them,' he tells his mother, ''till my arm aches. By my sword and valour, I could often kill them! Think, O my mother! – El Islam is menaced, armed infidels have set foot in our land, and these men, Muslims, will not learn their exercises.'[88] In the end a group of peasant soldiers turn on him and quietly murder him in cold blood.

But the central theme remains the position of women. Men in Egypt, Pickthall shows, have a political and economic monopoly of power in public. In the home this monopoly is circumscribed by the force of personality of women and by property rights safeguarded in the marriage contract. The wife has legitimate recourse to Islamic law: a law, however, which is codified and interpreted by men. Pickthall describes all this sympthetically but he does not turn away from injustices that arise from subordination. The benign Pasha corrects one of his wives by beating her. The unequal sexual opportunities for men lead to psychological cruelty. Even the outrageous injustices are explained away or accepted by his female characters. In strife, an older woman explains, 'is it not well that womanhood should be kept sacred and aloof, respected in the strife of Muslims – the ark which bears the future of the Faith?'[89] Women are numbered among the quiet folk. Yusuf furtively takes a second wife and also concubines. Another woman explains, 'It is the nature of men to have more wives than one, and a woman should no more resent his doing so – always provided he does not defraud her – than blame a cat for having several kittens at a birth.'[90]

The position of women in Islamic countries was much criticized by westerners. It still is. Pickthall does not whitewash. He justifies the standing of women on liberal Islamic grounds. Pickthall's ideal Muslim, enlightened, educated and tolerant, will be the head of a harmonious household. But even the idealized Pasha, from a sense of duty, flogs his wife. And in a community of ideal Muslims there would be no strife from which to protect womanhood. As far as it is possible to tell, Pickthall's picture of Cairene women a century ago is accurate. Other western perspectives have often been sentimental, tendentious, inaccurate, ignorant or unimaginative. Pickthall's work is a piece of anthropological observation. It is not easy to verify the facts of the social behaviour he reports. But he is taking advantage of the privilege of fiction in recording what is essentially true. *Veiled Women* is also a propaganda novel. It marks a further milestone on Pickthall's road to total identification with the world of Islam. If it does not convince, it explains much and, like his other Near Eastern novels, sheds light on practices and attitudes that are nowhere else so articulately recorded.

──────── *THE HOUSE OF WAR* (1916) ────────

The House of War was published in February 1916 when Pickthall had already been writing for several years in defence of Turkey and criticizing Christian missionary work in the Ottoman Empire. The House of War, he explains in a prefatory note, is 'the designation given formerly to all those Christians of the countries conquered by the Muslims who declined to embrace El Islâm'.[91] Missionary activity had unwittingly contributed to placing Ottoman Christians in a house of war in a wider sense. The novel shows how.

Elsie Wilding is the young niece of two maiden ladies who have had a quiet mission school in a Syrian town for thirty years. The ladies are unpretentious and unambitious. They defer to the British Consul, respect local society and invite the local Turkish governor, Hasan Pasha, to the school's prize-day. Elsie comes to stay with them. She has the passion of an English evangelist and considers her aunts to be lukewarm in their faith and compromising in their conduct. With her faithful, pert, doting servant, Jemileh, Elsie aspires to rent a house in a Christian village. Her independent efforts turn into a black comedy leading to disaster.

When Elsie moves into her village house, such is the novelty of an English woman living alone in such a place that people flock and squat in her garden, offending her sense of private property. Jemileh persuades her to be gracious and suggests a time for receiving visitors personally. A young Christian shaykh, Bekîr, who has acquired some English, pleases her but she finds his hangers-on uncouth. Her feelings are conveyed to Bekîr who 'had given no thought to his adherents until now, nor questioned the inherent right of everyone who wished to do so to bear him company'.[92] But the concession of an audience to Bekîr alone causes the murmur of scandal. She is obliged to admit Bekîr and his followers.

She arranges for a clinic to be opened, with professional assistance from the town. She helps the visiting nurse. But it does not please the faithful Jemileh 'that her mistress on whose dignity her own depended, should thus degrade herself before the eyes of'[93] the Christian village.

Elsie becomes bolder and decides to preach in a Muslim village. Jemileh objects, the Consul protests, the Turkish governor gently remonstrates. Elsie is adamant and, with the conviction of the insensitive, preaches the gospel to a gathering of incredulous Muslims. The terrified Jemileh explains that her mistress has a fit and the villagers accept this, and the shaykh entertains the two young women. Elsie sees her efforts as a success and repeats her visits and her preaching. The villagers come to listen because they are amused at her kitchen Arabic.

But poor Elsie's work is upsetting the delicate harmony that has existed between the Muslim village and the Christian village. The priest, Anton, feels cheated. Talk spreads that the privileged role of Christians has enabled Elsie to assail and insult the religion of Muslims. Rumour leads to tension and tension to incidents that include the killing of a child. This results in the prospect of war between the villages, averted only by the arrival of the governor with a troop of Turkish soldiers. Elsie learns the impolicy – if not the error – of her ways and happily falls in love with a friend of her brother, Dick Fenn, who fortuitously turns up just before the clashes.

The novel is not one of Pickthall's best. People turn up unexpectedly, individuals are sometimes caricatures. But there are a lot of good things in it. The events of the novel, one guesses, take place in the decade before 1914. Details of social nuances abound. When the Pasha attends the mission school prize-giving 'one or two native Christians who were in the room hurriedly resumed the headdress which they had discarded among Europeans'.[94]

Elsie finds her personal salvation in the arms of Dick Fenn, a man who comes out with the views of Pickthall himself. He lectures Elsie on the mistaken views of missionaries and the Islamic record of tolerance. When Elsie argues the need for good works and the salvation of souls, Fenn argues that the Muslim villagers are 'behind, but not below' us. He 'cannot see that you or I have been appointed over them'.[95]

The Turkish governor, Hasan Pasha, is another example of Pickthall's idealized wise upper-class Turk. He knows French in which language he reads Gibbon. He is a 'white-bearded man, immaculately clad in European fashion'. Elsie is disappointed at his appearance. 'She had expected something picturesque and barbarous, more evidently wicked than this neat old gentleman, who, but for his fez, might easily have been mistaken for a French diplomatist.'[96] When he chides Elsie about her activities, he does not mention religion but simply talks of the privileges she enjoys and which she might be abusing.

The novel is propaganda. Collectively, the Christians of the Ottoman Empire are not presented in a good light. They are grasping and cynical. When they acquire European ways they become figures of fun. The Turkish Muslims are the wronged ones. In the words of Fenn, 'The Turks neither offer nor expect apologies. They are too proud. They never even plead their case before the world. The native

Christians make the most of theirs. Always remember that when you hear the Turks accused.'[97]

And that of course was the message of Pickthall's wartime journalism.

KNIGHTS OF ARABY (1917)

Knights of Araby was subtitled 'A Story of the Yaman in the Fifth Islamic Century'. 1917, the year of the Russian Revolution and of Passchendaele, was hardly a propitious year in which to transport readers of novels to eleventh-century Yemen. But in his foreword Pickthall explains that his novel is an attempt to 'quicken those dry bones of memory, and reinvest them with some comeliness of flesh and blood. Even if unsuccessful, it may have the merit of calling the attention of the English reader to the fact that Muslims, all those centuries ago, confronted the same problems which we face today.'[98]

Knights of Araby takes place mainly in Zabid during the time of Sulayhid dominance. Two generations of the Sulayhid family appear in the novel: Ali and his proud wife Asma bint Shihab and their easy-going son, al Mukarram Ahmad and his wife Arwa, but called by Pickthall and the sources he used, al Sayyida, The Lady. The Sulayhids came from Manakha but held Sana'a as their capital before moving to Jibla. Their authority was upheld in the mountains by shifting alliances with other princelings. From time to time they occupied the coastal plain, the Tihama, and its principal city, Zabid.

The central historical figures in the novel are, however, members of the Najahid family, originally Abyssinian freedmen, who ruled Zabid in alternation with the Sulayhids. The fortunes of two brothers over a decade are traced: Saïd and Jayyash. Saïd, the elder, is called Al Ahwal, the Squinter, and is impetuous and ruthless. Jayyash is gentler, more scholarly, a lover of chess and the author of a history of Zabid.

The novel opens with the Najahids on the Red Sea island of Dahlak. The novel tells the tale of their capture of Zabid, losing it and taking it again. Pickthall's source for the novel was a collection of chronicles of medieval Yemeni history, published in English and Arabic in 1892. The major chronicle was that of Najm al-Din 'Umara al-Hakami (1135–73). His chronicle included fragments of Jayyash's own history of Zabid. Pickthall loved 'Umara and often referred to the work. "Umara', he wrote in 1931, 'did for a small corner of al-Yaman ... what many writers did for Baghdâd, Cairo, and Damascus, giving a picture of a period so vivid as to bring it near to us and make the actions of the folk intelligible to us today.'[99] 'The gossiping historian of the wars between Zabid and Sana'a,' as he called him on another occasion,[100] wrote a chronicle that was analysed by Ibn Khaldun. This analysis also appeared in the volume that was edited and translated by Henry Cassels Kay.[101]

It is clear that Pickthall worked on the Arabic rather than on Kay's translation. For example, before al-Mukarram Ahmad takes Zabid he addresses his troops and quotes the poet al-Mutanabbi, which Kay translates as:

> Grasping my death-dealing sword, I will go down among my
> foes,
> A field whence only they return who deal effective blows.[102]

Pickthall makes no attempt to put this into rhyme. His rendering is both simpler and more accurate:

> I go down, with my sword in hand, to waters
> Whence none return save by force of arms.[103]

To illustrate Pickthall's technique let us look at one passage from the novel and then the passage from the chronicle of 'Umara that Pickthall used. Twenty or thirty similar examples could be chosen. Al-Mukarram has taken Zabid in AH 475 where his mother is held prisoner.

> A knight in armour rode full tilt across the palace square and at the street-end reigned his horse and looked about him; then he proceeded slowly to the mansion of the severed heads. Two other horsemen followed at full gallop, overtaking him as he drew up beneath the lattice from which the Lady Asma leaned intent.
> He cried: 'May God perpetuate your honour, sovereign Lady!' His two companions proffered the same greeting each in turn. She replied in each case:
> 'Welcome, noble Arab!'
> She then inquired of the first rider: 'What is thy name?'
> 'My name,' he said, 'is Ahmad son of Ali son of Muhammad.'
> 'Among the Arabs there are many Ahmads sons of Ali. Have the goodness to disclose thy face to me.'
> The knight pushed up his visor. She exclaimed with pride: 'Welcome to thee, O our sovereign Lord Mukarram! Who are thy companions?'
> 'This, upon my right, is Al Karam the Yamite, and this, upon my left, is Aâmir Ez-Zawâhi.'
> 'Upon Al Karam I bestow the revenues from Aden for the

present year; to Aâmir I assign the fortresses of Kaukabân and Jaubân, with jurisdiction over all their territories. The grants are near of equal value, I think.'[104]

That little bit of drama is derived from a passage in 'Umara which Kay has translated thus:

> The first warrior to reach the spot where the two heads were set up, and to stand below the casement of Asmā, daughter of Shihāb, was her son, al-Mukarram Ahmad. He said unto her, and she did not recognize him, 'May God safeguard and perpetuate thy renown, O our Lady.' 'Welcome,' she replied, 'O noble Arab!' Al-Mukarram's two companions saluted her in the same words as his. She asked him who he was, to which he answered that his name was Ahmad, son of 'Aly son of Muhammad. 'Verily the name Ahmad son of 'Aly,' she answered, 'is borne by many Arabs. Uncover thy face that I may know thee.' He raised his helmet, whereupon she exclaimed, 'Welcome, our Lord al-Mukarram!'
> At that moment he was struck by the wind, a shudder passed over him, and his face was contracted by a spasm. He lived many years thereafter, but continued subject to involuntary movements of the head and spasms in his face. She then asked who were his two companions, and he named them. Upon one she conferred a grant of the revenues of Aden for that year, amounting to one hundred thousand dinārs. To the other she gave the two fortresses of Kaukabān and Haubān (?), together with their territories, the assessments upon which are not inferior to the revenues of Aden.[105]

There are significant differences in the two versions. Pickthall does not disclose the identity of the soldier who first greets the captive queen. We learn with Asma. Pickthall has no authority for naming the two companions who, we learn from an earlier paragraph of 'Umara, were with al-Mukarram Ahmad in the campaign. But naming them gives a smack of authenticity. The twitches and spasms of al-Mukarram are given a melodramatic twist by Pickthall. Al-Mukarram had waited for nearly two years before getting round to rescuing his mother. He was shaken out of his lethargy by a letter Asma smuggled to him (in a loaf of bread) saying that she was pregnant by Saïd the Squinter. Come and rescue me. The letter with its contents was a deceptive ruse. In *Knights of Araby* al-Mukarram's spasms occur only after he learns how his mother has deceived him. He is mortified, massacres half the population of Zabid in abstracted fury and hardly ever speaks to his mother again.

Rival royal households are not the exclusive stuff of the novel. There is in Zabid a gallery of personalities – some based on historic people, others completely invented. We have the jester, Abu Dad, who becomes, reluctantly and accidentally, a favoured courtier of both royal households. He longs to retire to a remote village and give up being forced to make jokes. There is the sinister Shaykh Salama, a dealer in girls and poisons, based on a person 'Umara writes about, but who lived in the following century. We have the saints, the scholars, the showmen, the marriage-brokers, the cameleers.

Zabid is described as a city of learning. 'History, geography, astrology, literature, medicine, besides, and in conjunction with, religious law, were deeply studied in its mosques and colleges by men whose names were known throughout the Muslim world. The doctors of Zabîd were Sunnite to a man; indeed the city was a tower of orthodoxy; yet the heretics consulted them on points of doctrine, and sent their children to be educated in their schools.'[106] The people of Zabid sway with whatever regime wields temporary power with a preference for Jayyash. They are among Pickthall's quiet folk.

'What are they in the sight of Allah?' said a great professor, when a student asked him wherefor, in his history of a certain country, he made no mention of its kings and famous warriors. 'They come and go. It is of infinitely more importance to record the sayings of the learned, the achievement of the poets and men of letters, the example of the pious and the growth of mosques and schools, which long endure.'[107]

War is the selfish activity of rulers, chiefs, great ones. As one shaykh of Zabid puts it:

'Ye know the saying of the Prophet (may God bless and save him): "Vengeance for blood is forbidden from henceforward, and the feud of blood practised in the days of the Ignorance is abolished." All men know that vengeance for blood is unlawful, yet look at all the country of the Arabs. The chiefs both great and small are all at feud. It is among the learned and the common people that the precepts of our faith have taken root and flourished. I say, those great ones, self-exalted, and their doings, are of small importance. They are lauded only by their slaves and their paid flatterers. The people as a whole endure them, while the learned hold them in contempt.'[108]

At another council of the Zabid 'ulama, another shaykh makes a similar point. 'The more that are indifferent to change of rulers, so only that each ruler be a Muslim, the better for Islam and the world at large; since fanatical attachment to one chieftain or one spot of ground, and hatred of another, is the cause of half the evils which affect mankind. The quiet folk are brothers in all lands. What part have they in the contentions of the proud?'[109] This was Pickthall's own view. Eight years after *Knights of Araby* he drew attention to the fact that the 'ulama watched over the welfare of the people, preserved Islamic culture and 'even forced Muslim rulers, in their un-Islamic strife',[110] to refrain from involving ordinary people in their squabbles.

Knights of Araby is clearly influenced by the 1914–18 war. It was published two months before Pickthall's public declaration of Islam. As in none of his other novels, all the characters are Muslim. Their terms of reference are exclusively Islamic. There is no problem of adjustment to the values and patterns of life of others. This is in contrast to all his other Near Eastern novels which directly and (more often) indirectly touch on the challenge caused by the cultural, economic penetration by western Europe of the Near East in the nineteenth and twentieth centuries.

As in his translation of the Qur'an, Pickthall is expounding the idea of Islam to an English-reading world. He is not overtly evangelical. But he was aware of unfavourable western interpretations of Islamic practices and attitudes, for example, of the role of women. On more than one occasion in *Knights of Araby* he goes out of his way to explain. 'Outside the polity of El Islam women were despised and badly treated. In the hands of the slave-dealers, also, they were liable to blows and insults. Once incorporated in the Muslim world by purchase, women had rights secured to them by law, and were respected.'[111]

The final lines of the novel tell of the pacific warrior, the passionate scholar, King Jayyash, going on the pilgrimage. Pickthall himself never performed the obligation of the pilgrimage. He was planning in 1931 to do so with a son of the Nizam of Hyderabad. The plan was abandoned because of an epidemic in the Hijaz arising from the outbreak of plague in the Yemen. There is thus a tragic irony in the serene and intense words describing Jayyash's first sight of Mecca:

Lines from the ancient poets thronged his memory like voices half awake before the dawn – the dawn of El Islam, of truth and light. The day was breaking. Far away across a land whose dust was hallowed by the persecuted footsteps of God's messenger, he saw the cruel, the beloved city in a glow. It was the blessing, and had been the curse, of El Islam – this city which contained no relic save its ancient memories of cruel persecution and idolatry; no beauty to seduce men's thoughts from God. And, as he pondered on the glory of the Unity, and how the folk of old obscured its light with vain imaginings, he praised the wisdom which had made men pilgrims to an empty house.[112]

————— *ORIENTAL ENCOUNTERS* (1918) —————

Oriental Encounters, subtitled 'Palestine and Syria (1894–5–6)', was a reprint of articles that appeared in the *New Age* between February 1917 and August 1918, with a few more tales added. It was reissued by Heinemann in the Travellers' Library in 1929 and is the best introduction to Pickthall's work. The book is a fictionalized account of his adventures and experiences, with some of the tales he heard during his travels in Syria. These impressions were 'clear after the lapse of more than twenty years. A record of small things, no doubt; yet it seems possible that something human may be learnt from such a comic sketch-book of experience which would never be derived from more imposing works.'[113]

Although the book was prepared for publication at a time of personal stress and of other preoccupations, it is full of freshness and high spirits. The three hundred pages of the first edition contain about twenty separate incidents, generally unrelated one to the other, but all disclosing Pickthall's first encounters with the Near East, his alienation from his fellow-Englishmen and his affection for the people of Syria and Palestine. Franks, usually Englishmen and often clergymen, are seen as intruders in the land, fair game for unscrupulous exploitation. This leads the foreigner to see the Syrian as covetous, devious and dishonest. Pickthall smiles genially at the encounters and slowly discards his own European perspective, thanks to his two remarkable companions, Rashid and Suleyman.

Rashid appears first as a soldier whom Pickthall buys out of the Ottoman army for five Turkish pounds. Rashid has tried to defraud Pickthall but becomes devoted to him, offering his services: 'By Allah, I can shoe a horse and cook a fowl; I can mend garments with a thread and shoot a bird upon the wing.'[114] He travels with Pickthall and when they settle at a village becomes an accomplished borrower of household necessities. 'He also did the cooking and the marketing without a hitch, giving a taste of home to the small whitewashed chamber,which we had rented for a week, it might be, or a month at most.'[115]

Suleyman was by profession, a dragoman, a guide to the western tourists who were coming to the Holy Land in increasing numbers. He earned enough in two months to maintain a wife and family in a

coastal village near Tyre. He was 'a man of decent birth, but poor
... who had acquired a reputation for unusual wisdom'.[116] The
more prosaic Rashid saw him 'as a famous liar, is our wise man
yonder; yet he speaks the truth!'[117] Suleyman often joined Pickthall
and Rashid and tells the best tales, some of which are far-fetched, but
all of which have a moral point. Some were traditional folktales and
were familiar to Pickthall's friend, J.E. Hanauer, and appear in
Folklore of the Holy Land.[118]

During his travels Pickthall often wore local dress. This at once
created a distance between him and other Englishmen. When
Pickthall tries to explain in English a point of custom to a strange
English tourist, he is met with: '"What! Are you English?" was his
only answer, as he scanned my semi-native garb with pity and
disgust.'[119] The same man, a missionary, is heavily patronizing, sees
Pickthall's youthful enthusiasm as a wayward fad and entertains him
for a meal in his tent. Pickthall rejoins Suleyman and some villagers.
'Looking round upon these eager, friendly faces, I compared them
with the cold face of the missionary, who suddenly appeared to me
as a great bird of prey. I hated him instinctively, for he was like a
schoolmaster; and yet his words had weight, for I was young to
judge, and schoolmasters, though hateful, have a knack of being in
the right.'[120]

Recent experience of an undistinguished school career makes the
young Pickthall vulnerable to scorn from his fellow-countrymen.
Other Englishmen patronize him after his fruitless attempt to
purchase property. He was urged 'to cheer up, for they had all been
through it'.[121] It, being presumably, affection for people of the land,
affection which age and wisdom turn to distance and disdain.
Disdain was often mutual, even though the intruding Englishmen
may be unaware of it. '"I never touch their food",' a missionary
explains. '"It is insanitary" – which I knew to be exactly what they
said of his.'[122]

Pickthall's memories tell us much of the provincial Syria in the
1890s. The government is to be avoided or its agents propitiated.
Authority is great, and small folk can only petition. Pickthall calls on
a provincial Ottoman governor. His anteroom is full of squatting
suitors. 'Some of these appeared so poor that I admired their
boldness in demanding audience of the Governor.'[123] The crowds
'sat or squatted round the walls in perfect resignation, some of them
smoking, others munching nuts of various kinds, of which the shells
began to hide the floor adjacent to them. A few of the suppliants had
even had the forethought to bring with them full bags of provisions,
as if anticipating that the time of waiting might endure for several
days.'[124]

We have the customary shrewd appreciation of detail revealing changes in social attitudes or behaviour. Services are developed for European tourists. Hotels, presuming to cater for European tastes, are springing up, run usually by Syrian Christians. One was 'a real hotel with table d'hôte, hall-porter, and a palm-lounge – everything, in fact, excepting drains'.[125] Another is called Howard's Hotel by the proprietor, Iskender Awwad, who has transformed himself into Alexander Howard.

Pickthall savoured those features that differed from his own English upbringing. He mocks the aspirations of Arab Christians when they adopt European habits, dress or pretensions and is unaware of the contradiction of riding around in Syrian dress scorning the Syrian who wears a parody of European dress.

There is a rosy romanticism in his landscapes, in his settings of dreamy Syrian villages. One such place 'was high up beneath the summit of a ridge, and from a group of rocks within a stone's throw of it could be seen the sea, a great blue wall extending north and south. We perched among the rocks, to watch the sunset.'[126] But the rosiness is kept in check. Elsewhere he meets a man of the desert who 'passed me a rough leathern water-bottle, and I took a draught of warmish fluid tasting like the smell of goats'.[127]

Oriental Encounters is high-spirited and also funny. His Europeans and Americans in Palestine are nearly all bizarre, not least one American admiral, on shore for two days only, who 'asked only one thing: to be shown the tree on which Judas Iscariot had hanged himself, in order that he might defile it in a natural manner and so attest his faith'.[128] And the tale, 'Bastirma', tells the story of . . . but a summary will spoil it for the prospective reader.

The book demonstrates Pickthall's preference for fiction as a vehicle for truth. It is not easy to tell the difference between reality and fancy. Conversations are obviously an imaginative reconstruction but Pickthall avoids specificity about placenames.

Oriental Encounters is remarkable in presenting events at three historical levels. First there are the fictionalized happenings of the 1890s, based presumably on memory stimulated by diaries or notebooks. These events reveal the Pickthall of the 1890s. Secondly there is the middle-aged man recalling important events of his youth with only a little condescension. He records his younger self with impulses and instincts that were checked by the orthodoxy of his elders. And thirdly there are his values of 1917–18 which coincide with what we know from his other writings. But his anger, bitterness and sadness are kept in rein.

There is another link between the two periods, a link that relates to Pickthall's psychological development. In 1894 Pickthall's career hopes were thwarted twice. He went to Palestine depressed and thinking he was a failure. The Syrian travels gave him a new perspective and helped him pick up the pieces of his life. And all this was an anticipation of the crisis of the years after 1914 which was resolved by his public acceptance of Islam. Thus *Oriental Encounters* records the way out of his first major personal crisis and was prepared for publication as he was resolving his second personal crisis. The passage of twenty-odd years has given him detachment – a detachment that allows him to display irony at the expense of himself, his ideas and his fellow-countrymen. Indeed the joyfulness of the book is, paradoxically, an outcome of depression and anguish. Pickthall gained from the catharsis. And so do his readers.

—————— THE EARLY HOURS (1921) ——————

The Early Hours was the last novel that Pickthall published. It is a novel with a cause. It presents the case for the Young Turks that Pickthall had been making for the previous eight years elsewhere. He is using the medium of propaganda with which he is most at home – fiction.

In 1921 the Young Turks, the allies of the defeated Germans, had few friends in Britain. The old prejudices about Turks and their unfavourable pre-war image were reinforced by the stigma of defeat. Not only were they wicked, they were also unsuccessful. Parts of western Anatolia were occupied by Greek invaders who had been egged on by the British Prime Minister. The Turkish national movement and the work of Mustafa Kemal Atatürk had not yet transformed the popular concept of the Turk. Thus the argument of *The Early Hours* had few potential sympathizers. There is however nothing defensive or bitter about the book. It is remarkably bright and has passages of great beauty.

Pickthall had already embraced Islam when the book was written. The cheerfulness of the novel reflects the new serenity in Pickthall's own life. Its title is taken from the *sura* of the Qur'an revealed to the Prophet at the lowest ebb of his fortunes. When Pickthall gave a sermon in 1919 on the text of this *sura* he drew comfort from the impermanence of misfortune. The years since 1913 had been dark years for Turkey and for Muslims, but Pickthall is sustained by hope and the precedent of the dark days of the Prophet. 'By the early hours,' he quoted as the theme of the book, 'and by the night when it is darkest, thy Lord has not forsaken thee nor does he hate thee.'[129] It was up to Muslims to do their duty, to educate their ignorant brothers and sisters and to complete that work of reform within the context of Islam upon which the young Turks had embarked.

The Early Hours tells the story of Camruddin, a young former soldier in the Turkish army between 1908 and 1913. Camruddin comes from Thrace and goes to Salonika and falls by chance into the company of young officers who are members of the Committee of Union and Progress. He finds a former patron, Sâdik Pasha, a conservative supporter of the old regime who redeems his promise of patronage to Camruddin by betrothing him to Gul-raaneh, a spirited and well-educated slave companion to the women of Sadik's household.

Camruddin is, again by chance, selected by Young Turk conspirators to take a message to Niazi Bey, a general in inland Macedonia. He is won over to the Young Turk cause and joins the revolutionary army of Niazi as it progresses through the hills and villages of Macedonia. The month is July 1908. The Sultan is forced to accept the demands of the revolutionaries, the constitution is proclaimed and reforms implemented.

Camruddin returns to the capital on a mission and secures a job in the Ministry of War. The events of four months take up two thirds of the novel. The last third follows the fate of Camruddin over the following five years. Camruddin marries Gul-raaneh. He joins the army of Mahmud Shevket which comes to Istanbul to crush the counter-revolution of 1909. He is at work, as a junior officer, in the suppression of brigandage at Bursa. When he is at the capital he studies English and French. We have glimpses of the fears, hopes and expectations of his friends who range from the foppish aristocrat, Ferid Bey, to the earnest Armenian supporter of the revolution, Dikram Bey.

He spends two years in Macedonia and on the outbreak of the Balkan wars in 1912 volunteers again for military service. The armies of the Balkan states overrun Thrace where his own wife and children have settled. Camruddin is injured, loses an arm and is back at the capital when he hears of the savage massacre of his family, betrayed by a Christian neighbour. The widowed daughter of Sâdik Pasha proposes marriage to the crushed Camruddin. The hero of the counter-revolution, Mahmud Shevket, is assassinated and the story ends with the newlywed couple, both past their youth, consoling themselves with the *sura* that gives the novel its title.

Pickthall's portrayal of Camruddin is a controlled development of the kind of person he has created before – the humble ordinary unspectacular young Muslim. Unlike Saïd the Fisherman or Mabrûk in *The Children of the Nile* he is not an unscrupulous opportunist. His Islam is profounder. Like a good Muslim he constantly praises God for the blessings of the world. He marvels at the beauty of nature, 'arranged, it seemed, with art for man's enjoyment'.[130]

The politics of Turkey are quietly woven into the background. As the novel proceeds Camruddin becomes more and more a partisan of the Unionists among the Young Turks. The cause of the revolution is summed up in the exhortation of Niazi to his troops in the hills: 'Build schools, instruct your people and repair your mosques.'[131] Camruddin observes the effects of the revolution while in the Bursa area. 'On every hand he heard the cry for education, sanitation, and improvements of all kinds. In many places schools were being built, the gift of rich men who approved the new ideas; and, meanwhile, lessons of the middle sort were given by old-fashioned khôjas in the mosques, who studied hard and anxiously, learning themselves the subjects which they taught their pupils.'[132] Camruddin's observations are of course those of Pickthall himself. In *With the Turk in Wartime* and in his articles in the *New Age* Pickthall repeatedly draws attention to the reforms carried out by the Young Turks, reforms that were unglamorous, that did not concern Anglo-Turkish relations but that were of immense significance to ordinary Turks. 'The Young Turks,' as one recent historian of modern Turkey has put it, 'may have failed to give Turkey constitutional government. They did, however, give Istanbul drains.'[133]

There are other echoes of Pickthall's journalism. In November 1914, he wrote how 'Niazi Bey and Enver Bey took to the mountains, each with a little band of *fedais* sworn to free the country or to die ... Niazi Bey, that single-minded servant of ideas ... addressed his two hundred followers at the crossroads on the green height above Resna bidding all those who were faint of heart to leave him.'[134] As in *Knights of Araby* Pickthall uses the licence of the novelist to add a number of touches. The troops climbed the hill over Resna, 'following in single file a winding path which traversed a dense undergrowth of scented shrubs with here and there a group of forest trees'.[135] At the summit, the 'men piled arms, loosed belts, and flung themselves upon the ground, plucking the grass and looking out over the sunny land'.[136]

When at the Turkish capital Camruddin, like Pickthall in 1913, lived at Erenköy, the prosperous Asiatic suburb. As Pickthall had done, Camruddin used

> to set out along a shady avenue which led him shortly to a railway station bowered in foliage. The train then carried him to Haïdar Pasha, whence a steamer bore him over laughing waters to the bridge of Ghalata, which spans the entrance to the Golden Horn. There was always the same crowd of men upon the train and steamboat, who came to know each other and converse as friends.

Each person carried in his hand his chosen newspaper, which he perused in the intervals of conversation, of which the subject was invariably politics ... Arriving at the Bridge, his first concern, as that of everybody was to have his boots cleaned of the dust of the surburban roads.[137]

Political and religious commitment add an intensity to this novel. As in the other Near Eastern novels we are invited to see the world as Camruddin sees it. A Turkish bey, educated in France, invites Camruddin to lunch. The meal was set forth 'in the Frankish manner on a table raised so high above the ground that everybody had to sit on chairs to get at it'.[138] Pickthall's identification with Camruddin is closer than with any other of his creations. The hopes Camruddin expressed for a reformed Turkey are Pickthall's hopes. Camruddin's quiet faith in the face of adversity resembles that of Pickthall's newly adopted Islam. Camruddin was happy as an ordinary soldier. Pickthall was content as a private and then a corporal at the end of the First World War. The contentment of each was derived from his faith. And Camruddin's views on marriage echo directly those of his creator. Camruddin tells his wife that the 'soul of every living man and woman is solitary from the cradle to the grave ... Your mind and soul, and mine, are independent of each other. But we are travelling the same road, we are servants of the same Lord.'[139]

The Early Hours has thus elements of autobiography. It forms part of the process whereby Pickthall sought to identify with Islam and Asia by becoming one of them. He and Camruddin, in spite of their different personal histories, have one mind with the same views and the same hopes. As in his religious writings, the language is simpler than in his earlier novels. Pickthall has a message to convey. The passion and the absence of irony reflects the serene earnestness that inspired him to devote the rest of his life to the service of Islam.

6.

TALES OF ENGLAND AND EUROPE

'. . . one of the least changed of our counties . . . for
the peasantry still speak old English with an ancient
accent, and keep up customs long disused.'

Pickthall on Suffolk[1]

—— THE REST OF THE SHORT STORIES ——

In each of the three volumes of short stories the tales are divided into
three sections based on the location of each tale. Most deal with the
Near East, but seven are sited in Switzerland and twenty-one take
place in England, usually in Suffolk.

In the tales concerning the English Pickthall is interested in themes
of class and place. The social range of class in his tales is wide, from
aristocrats to the destitute. He is not happy when dealing with the
very noble or the very wealthy but is more at home with the people
of his own class, respectable upper-middle-class folk living on
annuities for whom only a limited number of activities are
legitimate: the older professions for the men, domesticity for the
women. Some of them could not afford to stay in England. They came
to 'colonize Geneva and Lausanne from motives of economy. They all
went up to the mountains in the heat of summer, but could not afford
to pay the price of grand hotels. A price they could afford they paid
like clockwork.'[2] Within this class small distinctions signified much
in human relations.

His stories of lower-class life have a touch, but only a touch, of paternalism. He observes and records and sympathizes with peasant obstinacy. In a conflict between peasants and gentlefolk, the peasant, if he does not win, at least has the best lines.

Pickthall applauds the village community, local patriotism, particularism: the determination, for example, of one tiny Swiss village to triumph over another; the local beliefs scorned by the cosmopolitan world. 'Tell me,' asserts one character who has confidence in the powers of a mountain faith-healer, 'is it more extraordinary that a man of Vaud should find a charm to heal a Valaisan, than that my barometer should announce the storm while it is distant?'[3]

His English tales show sensitivity to the passage of time, to the break-up of an idealized rural community. 'Fifty years ago in every good-sized village in East Anglia there was a brewery, a ropewalk, a foundry, a rickcloth manufactory and two or three windmills; of which the ruins may be seen today . . . and their decay has much contributed towards the depopulation of rural districts where now a youth must till the soil or emigrate.'[4] The little village of Chillesford, where Pickthall spent his earliest years, used to have a windmill, a water-mill, a decoy with pipes and nets and dogs, and a brick kiln which produced bricks and slates. None save the water-mill remained in use by the First World War.[5]

Pickthall's uneducated Suffolk people use words and phrases of dialect and he has as keen an ear in recording this dialect as he had in learning Syrian Arabic. We find the drawn out adverb 'wholly', as in 'I fare whol-ly stammed';[6] 'mander' as in 'that warn't no mander o' use';[7] the vocative 'bo';[8] the mock-abusive 'duzzy ole fules' and the affectionate 'ye little mucks'.[9]

Pickthall was constantly conscious of a contrast between naturalism and sentimentality. Nature was good; it was the rule of God. Sentimentality was a flight from reality, a distortion of the truth. Loyalty to the point of stubbornness, loyalty to a place, an idea, a way of life, was wholesome and natural. Sentimentality included falsehoods arising from class distinctions and from religious practice. All these elements appeared in one short story, 'The Rising Tide', the last in the last volume published.[10]

In this tale the Briggs family has moved to Holly Grove, on the Chelmsford road. Mr Briggs is a bookish retired civil servant with two girls at home and a son at school at Rugby. His wife is the daughter of an energetic parson and 'did all the talking and she did it well'. She concerned herself with the poor. As a girl she had helped her father, 'thus acquiring in her youth the instinct of trained sheep-dogs for rounding up a flock wherever seen'.[11] She sets to work harassing the poor with Bible classes, sewing parties and clothing clubs. With the half-hearted help of local gentry she gets up a most ghastly entertainment, an evening of ill-prepared playlets, recitations of French songs and renderings of patriotic poetry. The show makes £5 and Mrs Briggs, undaunted by the fiasco, suggests spending it on missionary work and the local adoption of a little black boy.

'"I don't know as we're that fond o' blacks in Holly Grove," said Mrs Dawson thoughtfully.'[12] Mrs Dawson is the mistress of the village shop with some lively teenage children. When they protest at the ill manners of the Briggs, their mother tells them they can no more teach manners to the gentry '"than you can teach a steam-engine. You must just look on as you would at a play, say 'Sir and Ma'am', and mind you don't get hurt."'[13]

The son at Rugby, Jack Briggs, is the only one of the family, in the words of Mrs Dawson's daughter, May, 'that talks to you as if you were a human being'.[14] Mrs Briggs and the girls are away and May boldly invites Jack to a party. Jack thoroughly enjoys himself.

> As he said afterwards, there was no nonsense, everybody talked to everybody; a decent orchestra was going and some tophole grub. There must have been a hundred people present, and at least a score of couples always dancing. The Dawson girls took charge of him, and either danced with him or found him partners. He talked footer with the boys and hunting with old Dawson, and stayed entranced till half past two o'clock when he walked home gaily chatting with the Greenlands' lodge-keeper, his wife and daughter. He had not dreamt that village life was such good fun.[15]

Mrs Briggs, when she got back, was far from pleased 'deploring his transgression of an unseen boundary'. She explained, 'We must keep our distance or all our cultivated social life will be submerged in commonness.'[16] Jack found it 'just natural' but weakens when an appeal is made to his pride as a gentleman in the making. 'Seeing him waver, she attacked more strongly, appealing to his holiest sentiments, his better self, his love for home, his duty to his parents and his God; painting his father's grief, his sisters' shame; drenching him with the social poison in so sweet a form that he esteemed it sacred teaching, gospel truth.'[17]

Pickthall ends the tale on a note of unsentimentality. Illusion – and poison – triumph and Jack submits. The artificial restraints, class prejudices and hypocrisies, buttressed by the formal religion, are, for Jack, momentarily abandoned when he glimpses the natural world of peasants' merrymaking. 'The Rising Tide' was published when Pickthall had turned his back on the values of England and what he saw as her spurious and fragile class system, and had become a member of the fraternity of Islam.

———————— ALL FOOLS (1900) ————————

All Fools, 'being the story of some very young men and a girl', was published in June 1900. Pickthall's first novel is a frivolous tale of a group of young gentlefolk who are studying with a private tutor in London. After the success three years later of *Saïd the Fisherman* Pickthall disowned his first book, bought up copies and destroyed them. In his *Who's Who* entry *All Fools* is not recorded among his publications. The writing is often bad: wordy, laboured and facetious. There are a few, but only a few, indications of the talent or the seriousness of the later Pickthall.

The novel tells the story of Douglas Lee-Stretton, known as Bunny from his rabbit-like mouth, 'a young gentleman with pretensions to dandyism of a horsey kind'[18] and his half-hearted affair with the pert Millicent Woodward who lives with her bedridden mother and vulgar brother Percy. The first half of the novel deals with the kidnapping of Douglas by two stagey Germans and its consequences.

The novel changes tone halfway through. Bunny's fellow students include a comic Indian and a foppish aristocrat Blackstone. The Indian could be Billy Bunter's form-mate in *Magnet* and is mocked throughout the book. Blackstone however develops into a serious character. He falls in love with Millicent but behaves decently. He organizes the lives of others in a way quite inconsistent with the character of the Blackstone of the first hundred pages.

The writing really is bad. The novel's extended title suggests a greater age for the author than twenty-five years. Each chapter has a title which preciously recalls literary fashions of 1750: 'Chapter VII wherein the reader may, if he choose, observe the way of a very young man with a maid'. The novel is long, its length drawn out by such periphrases as: 'The door opened to admit of the passage of a human body.'[19]

Pickthall's understandable distaste for his first creation was probably due mainly to his extraordinarily grotesque portrait of the Indian, Baraoniji, known to officialdom as Boanerges and to his friends as Brown Geegee. He is seen as a simpleton with an incomplete grasp of the English language. He drinks whisky, is totally insensitive to the hearty jokes of which he is a butt. He is seen externally, through the eyes of insubstantial insular Englishmen. The reader is invited to dehumanize him on occasions, such as when 'he emitted a low, grating noise, like the snarl of a dog, exposing two rows of gleaming white teeth. He rolled his eyes, so that only the yellowish whites of them were visible.'[20] It is amazing to compare the unfortunate portrayal of the Indian with that of the Syrian fisherman, Saïd, three years later. Even more so when we bear in mind that Pickthall was writing both novels over the same period.

There are a few stray hints of a more reflective Pickthall, indications of powers of observation and social commentary. He describes, with effect but without affection, a newly built West Kensington road which

> was among the newest eruptions of that insidious disease of the earth's face – the bricks-and-mortar leprosy, which, fostered and fed abundantly by the mercantile spirit of the English, has crept so far and achieved so much that it has come to be considered as a national institution, and therefore as unassailable . . . The houses were small and semi-detached, with little strips of tasselated pavement leading from iron gate to dark-green door with brass handle and knocker. Each dwelling was of red-brick, and had an excrescence in the shape of a bow window built square out of deference to the architecture which was supposed to bear some mystic relation to Queen Anne through Kate Greenaway. There was something of the upstart in this Avenue, with its affected, lackadaisical gables and chimneys, sprung up as it were in defiance of the older, stuccoed growth of the street, terrace-gardens, and road by which it was on all sides beset.[21]

Another passage describing the fog of London presages Pickthall's ability to turn intense observation and reflection into imaginative prose. From a great height 'it would have seemed as if the houses, churches, and public buildings, the river with its many bridges and all the shipping of the Pool had been packed carefully for the night in cotton-wool, lest they should jostle against and break each other, as the world rolled on its course through space'.[22]

Pickthall also has flashes of insight into social changes – the insecure but changing status of women employed as typists in the city or the striving of the lower middle class for some security, the 'pitiful struggle after the shadow of gentility'.[23] Unlike the rest of his English novels, all the action takes place in an urban setting, in London.

But facetious satire sets the tone and inhibits social or psychological realism. Pickthall's later judgement of the work was sound. It remains of interest only for the promise it all but fails to show.

———————— ENID (1904) ————————

Enid is an intriguing novel to follow *Saïd the Fisherman*. So much of Pickthall's personality went into *Saïd*. By contrast *Enid* is a conventional novel of rural Suffolk, very much in an English literary tradition.

Enid herself is the younger daughter of a successful draper who comes to Suffolk and aspires to gentry status. The novel tells the story of four marriages: that of Enid herself, of her sister, of her maid, and the second marriage of her father. In each marriage there are moral and social crises that challenge the behaviour prescribed for the respectable classes. Enid elopes on impulse with her lover Sidney, a poet of solitary habits. The scandal of elopement is lessened when her family learn that Sidney is a gent. Intimacy however shows him up as a possessive, self-pitying bore. Enid leaves him to take lodgings at Easterwick, a coastal town that seems to be based on Southwold or Walberswick. (Pickthall had a step-sister, Caroline, who lived in Walberswick.) Sidney in despair hangs himself.

Enid's father, Simon Glover, the ex-draper, marries the youngish Honourable Mrs Hermia Garland who had in her youth imprudently eloped with the groom who, the family believe, was later drowned at sea. Mr Garland inconsiderately reappears to blackmail Hermia. But the crisis is averted when in the end it turns out that Mr Garland had always been a bad egg, being already married when he led Hermia astray. His first wife is still alive and so his marriage to Hermia is bigamous and invalid. Any children that Simon and Hermia have will be legitimate, which is good news for them, but bad news for Enid and her sister, Ruth, who has a joyless marriage with a tight-fisted army captain.

Enid's maid, Lottie, runs off with Hermia's brother, a languid viscount. In spite of misalliance – and Lottie has to be educated up to her new station – hers is the happiest marriage of them all.

The events of the marriages are narrated in a lively way and involve the mutual personal relations of all. But the personal interaction takes place within a rigid code of expected social behaviour and a tight hierarchy. When Enid elopes, the identity of her lover is unknown. The outrage of her family turns to satisfaction and even amused admiration when they learn that he is not, as was feared, another groom. 'I'm so relieved, I hardly mind'[24] says her father. Social rules are more rigid than moral rules. The viscount's marriage with the maid is concealed for over a year – two pregnancies notwithstanding – until Lottie has acquired sufficient social graces to play the lady. The reunion of Lottie and her awkward farm labourer brother is a sustained and contrived comic passage.

The faults of *Enid* are obvious: conventionalized behaviour, the writing for a readership that shared assumptions of the immutability and rightness of a social pattern of class deference and clientage. The gentry and the would-be gentry speak standard English, the lower classes are made to speak an authentic Suffolk dialect. The social condescension is embarrassing, sometimes mawkish.

Yet if we accept the pervasiveness of class distinctions in 1900 as we do when we read the works of Wells, Galsworthy or Bennett, we can recognize an acuteness of perception in Pickthall's treatment of passion and disillusion and the tyranny of convention. There is a contrast in behaviour that goes beyond the obviously comic. When the farm labourer, Chris Heaviland, wanders down to Wimbledon and calls on his sister, the viscountess, 'The softness of the mats was something awful, mysterious, religious for a man accustomed to rouse echoes where he trod.'[25]

Pickthall is not wooden in his characterization. We appreciate why his characters behave as they do. There is a skill as a story teller that keeps us alert, and surprises are sprung right to the end. He can tersely produce the shape and colour of places. Ipswich, for example, is described 'with its queer-shaped warehouses, chimneys, towers and steeples swathed in mist of lilac, a hue which the muddy river, mirroring the last of the sunset, held more clearly.'[26]

Near Eastern interests are kept under control. References to the East are as conventional as those of any fashionable author who had not been east or south of Italy. At one point, Sidney's thoughts 'ran riot like a horde of dervishes brandishing weapons and howling thanks to Allah'.[27] A moonlit night is 'full of charm and perfume like an Arabian treasure-cave'.[28]

Where Pickthall does show unusual merit is in his sensitivity to the vulnerability of respectable women or ladies. When Enid compromises herself by eloping, she has the choice of marriage or an ostracism which is relieved only

> by full and ceremonial submission, a torture of months and years comparable to that parade of the penitent of old in white shift, candle in hand, through a jeering mob to shrift and sanctuary. That way of absolution was too shameful to contemplate. Marriage remained as the yoke she must pass under to reinstatement in the good graces of the world so-called'.[29]

Submission, torture, yoke: it is the woman who is the victim.

This is the first of Pickthall's three Suffolk novels. Already in his twenties Pickthall reveals a nostalgia for an arcadian rural past: 'She was in a bend of one of those lanes with wide green margents and copse-like hedges, which tell of a boundless time when space was not economised as it is nowadays.'[30]

But it is a convincing Suffolk with its 'immensity of sky'[31] and its dialect. Just as we learn something of nineteenth-century Syria from *Saïd the Fisherman*, so *Enid* is a partial portrait of a rural Suffolk between the arrival of the telegraph and the advent of the motorcar.

BRENDLE (1905)

Brendle is the story of John Ashford, his family and his home town over the course of about ten years from 1884 to 1894. The Brendle of the title is the name of an East Anglian town, which, from internal evidence, would appear to be Woodbridge, Suffolk, about twelve miles from Pickthall's first home, Chillesford.

John Ashford is a widower, a prosperous brewer (like the family of the first wife of the father of Marmaduke) with control of five hundred public houses in the region. He is a churchwarden, Mayor of the town and the leading figure in Liberal Party politics. The novel relates the fortunes of his three daughters and two sons. One daughter, Mabel, marries the young Liberal Member of Parliament; another, Clara, weds the supine son of the snobbish Rector. The elder son, Hammond, has quarrelled with his father; the younger son is a feckless dilettante. John Ashford is a bullying autocrat and Hammond is made to work in the brewery for no pay. He quits and opens up his own design shop and marries a pretty schoolteacher called Jenny. A random selection of Brendle folk pass through the pages making not a great impression. Some of the MP's aristocratic relations and an Eton contemporary of Hammond, a wealthy and sybaritic Jew, Breitstein, make minor appearances.

The novel does not hold together well. There are too many characters. Some enticing themes are not developed, such as Hammond's own ideas. He is a follower of the Arts and Crafts movement, influenced by the writings of William Morris and John Ruskin. Hammond made his poor wife read 'books which confused her notions on right and wrong'.[32]

The character of John Ashford is overdrawn. He only comes alive on the day of his death when he meets his daughter-in-law, Jenny, and takes her to lunch at a Blackfriars hotel which he has used all his life. The hotel staff know him and he has used the hotel, it is hinted, for clandestine rendezvous in his more vigorous past.

The allusions to politics are suggestive. John Ashford's Liberalism has a religious reverence for Gladstone that parallels the faith of a Muslim. 'He prayed towards Hawarden.'[33] His personal loyalties to the Grand Old Man overcame reservations about Irish Home Rule. His son-in-law, Cyprian Wells, is elected Member of Parliament in 1886 but defects to the Conservatives six years later. John Ashford, aged seventy, becomes MP then but is shortly afterwards ennobled as Lord Brendle.

Pickthall shows his ear for Suffolk dialogue and demonstrates his ability to draw out the significant physical detail. And there are occasional shafts of humour such as his description of Major Bathurst – who resembles Dobbin in Thackeray's *Vanity Fair*: 'He thought as a soldier, looked like a soldier, spoke as a soldier. Even his attachment to Stephanie turned out soldierly – a kind of drill.'[34]

As in his other early novels there is a preciousness in his use of archaic words. On one page alone we have leaguer, marplot and moil. Such a use mystifies rather than clarifies.

A common theme in this, as in the other English novels, is preoccupation with social inequalities and the discord that follows the untuning of the string of social harmony. Marital misalliance is under strain from the pressures of public opinion and *Brendle* ends with Hammond and Jenny being separated. This relationship started with an awareness, certainly on Jenny's part, of social inferiority, even though there 'was nothing in his bearing to suggest that he accounted her of a lower class than himself'.[35] Hammond's sister saw 'Jenny rising, almost a lady, and our brother sinking, actually wishing to be a tradesman'.[36] The marriage of Jenny and Hammond, whose family are themselves patronized by Cyprian Wells, MP ('He had done wrong to look down on these brewing people')[37] 'struck at the social tranquillity of the town'.[38] The Rector is foremost in seeking to preserve the social harmony and threatens ostracism, 'If you get entangled with a girl beneath you,' he tells Hammond, 'we should have to – er – of course, to drop you.'[39]

Pickthall's own social background, with its brewing connections, had its ambiguities. His alternative life in the East is kept in check but is used to contrast the English life for which Pickthall had opted. One summer Hammond Ashford and some aristocratic friends go on a cruise to Smyrna. 'Brendle faded like a sea-fog left behind . . . These mountain-shores, distinct in every fissure, between opaque blue sea and jewel sky, manifested a reality far transcending that of March twilight brooding on a northern fenland.'[40] And on his return to England reality gives way to charm.

Coming from a land bare of mist, he discovered in the home

atmosphere a charm subtle and mysterious. It subdued and diffused the light, which shot everywhere yet was nowhere, like the lustre in a milky gem. He saw the Kentish fields and orchards defile through a wondrous twilight suffused with purple and amber and rose. The train rocked through Chatham, where the smoke flung blue ghost tresses up from shadowy chimneys. It roared on a bridge; when he beheld the square keep of Rochester guarding the grey ridge, at the bend of the river turned to blood by the sunset. What was the hard brightness of the Grecian isles compared to this witch twilight of the mystic fires?[41]

This is revealing. In spite of himself Pickthall is not adjusting to the life of a quiet country gentleman in England. The imagery associated with 'the east' is far more real than the abstractions of England where light was everywhere and nowhere with the witch twilight of mystic fires, whatever that means. England is the abode of woolly sentimentality.

Brendle is of limited interest for its own sake. It is a potboiler and lacks some of the subtlety of his first Suffolk novel, *Enid*, or the warmth of his last, *Larkmeadow*.

THE MYOPES (1907)

The title is not helpful. One is not sure how to pronounce it and it in no way illuminates the content. It seems to be a comment on the need to be far-sighted in human relationships and to avoid preoccupation with the immediate. But this is not clear.

Gertrude and Theodore are children brought up by an unworldly Norfolk bachelor vicar. Gertrude is his orphaned niece, Theodore the orphaned son of a woman the vicar had loved and who, 'preferring at the irrevocable hour a lighter gallant, had paid the penalty of her inexperience in misery, desertion, and an early grave'.[42] The two children grow up together, then move away from Norfolk and, though more intimate with their shared background than brother and sister, have no thought of marrying each other. Both embark on fraught and ultimately miserable marriages. Gertrude and her husband separate, Theodore's wife is intensely jealous of Gertrude. The jealousy drives Gertrude and Theodore into each other's arms and they elope from a Swiss hotel full of English. After a brief 'honeymoon' Gertrude awakes to the impossibility of a permanent relationship and they separate never to meet again. She is secretly kept by an admirer, Maurice, a smart and cynical lawyer. Theodore returns to his spouse and with her goes off to be 'vice-consul at an obscure and wellnigh defunct seaport on the confines of Syria and Asia Minor'.[43] Nobody lives happily ever after.

There are elements of Pickthall himself in Theodore. Both are brought up by East Anglian clergymen. Theodore as a young man goes on a commission to the Balkans. He wanders on to the Levant and on his return to England feels very much out of place, conscious of a gulf of difference between the world of the Near East and the world of Europe, 'Pleasure, love, all human interest there was objective always; here subjective. The gulf fixed had not always yawned so wide. The castle Chillon' – Theodore is reflecting in Switzerland – 'there below, knee deep in the lake as cattle stand, was of the old time, neighbour to the life he came from. It seemed one with the natural scene; whereas the modern ballet of hotels and villas, smirking, pretentious, was thrown up by the landscape as indigestible.'[44] Life in Europe is an anticlimax. *The Myopes* was written when ten years had passed since Pickthall had been in the east and they are passages of yearning. When Theodore returned later to the east he 'entered on a new lease of life and saw fun everywhere'.[45] All this had its parallels in Pickthall's experiences. *The Myopes* was published just after Pickthall had returned to Egypt where he acquired a new lease of life and saw fun everywhere. Theodore, like Pickthall, pays lip service to convention but is not part of the social whirl of English middle-class life.

The Myopes also explicitly records a barren view of marriage which was later to be absorbed into Pickthall's Islamic view of marriage, expressed by characters in his later Near Eastern novels (*Veiled Women, Knights of Araby* and *The Early Hours*) and in his Islamic writings. Intimacy in a marriage is a delusion. Gertrude, disillusioned in her marriage, counsels Theodore before his. 'By admitting anyone into your holy of holies,' she says, 'you bare your heart, and are liable to get hurt in quarrels which would otherwise be trifling. Therefore, I say, keep your past life to yourself, and respect hers as it were a secret. I don't suppose there ever were two people, bred as strangers, who were the better or happier for knowing every detail of each other's lives.'[46]

The Myopes has an undertone of disquiet. The social life Pickthall depicts in his earlier English novels is set off against the east. Such English life is absurd when it is exported to a Swiss hotel. But Pickthall outlines a comic situation and does not easily move from that to a sustained comic narrative.

There is humour but not comedy. We have examples of his ear for dialect, catchphrases and intonation. 'How are *you*, Mrs Moore,'[47] is the greeting of Whitley, the smug, affably radiant and vulgar colleague of Theodore in a city office. And Pickthall captures an upper-class attitude to women when Jack, the inane Bedfordshire squire, is made to regard women as two kinds, 'perfumed vice and breezy virtue . . . between which males might oscillate, but females never'.[48]

The Myopes is the last novel in which Pickthall describes in detail the conventional social world of his own background. His next novel, *Larkmeadow*, is a semi-autobiographical account of events in a Suffolk village; his last English novel, *Sir Limpidus*, is a send-up of the whole business of the social novel. In *The Myopes* Pickthall longs for the east. There are a few lines of description of the Syrian port where Theodore becomes the vice-consul – is it Iskenderun? – and we have the contrast between England on the one hand and the sands swirling over the town, 'the sight of many skeletons of dead animals, and sometimes a fresh carcase with the lean dogs tearing at it'[49], on the other. It is a dream, but not a nightmare. It is the world where Pickthall was at home, and such realistic detail is missing from his English novels.

—————— *LARKMEADOW* (1912) ——————

Larkmeadow, published in August 1912 by Chatto and Windus, a publishing house that Pickthall had not published with before – and was not to publish with again – is a story of rural Suffolk. It is based on his memories of residence at Holton in north-east Suffolk at the turn of the century. Suffolk people are like the people of the Near East in his novels. There is something solid, organic and authentic about them. Outsiders presume and blunder.

The blundering outsider in *Larkmeadow* is Mr Harraby Vasey, a retired solicitor, prosperous and confident, who has distant family connections in the village of Larkmeadow to which he retires. He treats the rural poor with condescension and expects gratitude and deference in return. 'Hitherto, he had known the lower orders, so to speak, only in captivity – horses between the shafts, well-trained and driven for him.'[50] The Suffolk rural peasantry had their own values, their own systems of deference and clientage. Vasey assumes leadership of the parish council and aspires to influence in the county and, indeed, is nominated as the Liberal parliamentary candidate. In the village of Larkmeadow he wishes to fence off some heathland which he believes belongs to him. And this leads to problems. Legally it is his property but custom is strong and the custom has been that children play on the heathland and villagers believe that there is a right of way across the land. When this popular custom is challenged, Vasey becomes unpopular in the village. He is seen as a 'slinkin' Cockney'[51] and thereafter can do no right. The novel follows the dispute with minor themes of the attitude of the members of his family and close friends. We have a rich cast of villagers, who take sides on Vasey's rights, and a wise farmer cousin whom Vasey absurdly and ineffectually patronizes.

Pickthall's sympathies are with the Suffolk peasant. 'A peasantry,' he wrote in 1927 when he was in India, 'has always common sense; it has no absurd pretensions, no false standards.'[52] In the case of the people of Larkmeadow he shows his observation of the language of north-east Suffolk, the turns of phrase, the dialect word and the vivid pronunciation. Suffolk logic is different from the imported logic of Vasey. Or as one character puts it, 'He don't fare to be able not to think straight like what we dew.'[53] Old customs are cherished. The villagers believe that a funeral procession over disputed land makes that land common. 'A bit of medieval folklore strayed into the twentieth century,'[54] as a visiting journalist puts it.

A leading light of the parish is a retired London policeman, originally of local origin, with the Suffolk name of Catchpole. He is an enthusiastic local politician who wishes to see far greater authority and autonomy given to the parish council. 'Why had the County Council all the power, the parish none? And why had every man a vote for Parliament, yet no control of what he knew and cared about?'[55] Catchpole's views are those of Pickthall himself who wrote three years later that it seemed to him 'the very basest form of cheating to give a man a vote for Parliament or the County Council and proclaim him a free citizen, while witholding from him all control of homely matters which he knows and cares about.'[56]

Just as the Near Eastern novels document the invasion of Europeans into a balanced if uncertain world of pious scallywags who shift according to their own social and moral codes, so rural Suffolk is invaded by urbanism. It is personified by Harraby Vasey but there are other aspects of the invasion. Pickthall was himself aware of the pull of the cities, the slow decline of rural crafts and village self-sufficiency. Pickthall has an idealized world of mutually dependent nobility, farmers and peasants: a Disraelian 'Young England' ideal. When Harraby Vasey is on one occasion worsted, he regrets he ever came to Suffolk and 'longed at that moment to be back at Wimbledon, in the circle of his old acquaintance, cultivated, wealthy people, equally remote from lords and farmers'.[57]

Part of the invasion consists of organized party politics. The wife of one peasant explains her husband's refusal to join the parish council: 'He don't hold wi' politics. He try to keep hisself respectable.'[58] And the subtle party politician, the Liberal agent, is another Disraelian creation. He is 'a man of dubious gentility, fluent, hard-voiced, positive, holding all things lawful which were not illegal'.[59] Politics brings in the press from London who exaggerate and caricature and for their own metropolitan ends distort the Larkmeadow conflict.

Larkmeadow is a nostalgic tale with a social moral. Pickthall is in complete command of his material and there is more discipline than in any of his other English novels. It is not a detached story. Pickthall is using the novel as a platform for his own views. He is recording a transition that he does not like. As a writer, a journalist and a cosmopolitan, as one who brought his own urban values to a remote village, he was part of the process of undermining the self-sufficiency of the blissful unlettered villagers. But as he said elsewhere of the traditional way of life of another Suffolk village, 'the schoolmaster is abroad; all this is passing away'.[60]

———————SIR LIMPIDUS (1919) ———————

Sir Limpidus is a strange novel. It tells the story of the career of a conventional and successful Liberal aristocratic politician. It is extremely readable and lacks the frivolity and lightness of his earlier English novels. There is a touch of Disraeli in the politics, a touch of Trollope in the social scenes.

Sir Limpidus FitzBeare is born in the 1860s, and we follow his life to the outbreak of war in 1914. His career is in some ways an ideal of aristocratic paternalism and seems to be a very gentle satire on the way British politics and society operate. The FitzBeares have ample estates, Limpidus' father is a loyal Liberal, proud of his Country, his Name and his Property (which brings in an income of £70,000 a year). He is kind to his tenants who repay the kindness with deference. He indulges them in drink and rough revels on occasions like the coming of age of his son and heir. Indeed he even 'revived the ancient English sport of grinning through a horse-collar'.[61] His politics are simple: 'I stick to my own side whatever happens,' he confided to his son. 'And I look at it like this: if the people are coming up (and the new franchise settles that), we'd better meet them half-way in a friendly spirit than oppose them.'[62] To his son's prospective constituents he presented his political philosophy in a different way. 'We've all jogged along together, gentle and simple, for centuries; and we aren't going to fly at each other's throats just because some half-baked counter-jumping townsman happens to come along and tells us a whole lot of fairy tales.'[63]

Limpidus absorbs such a political tradition together with other values of aristocratic conventionality. His view of virtue was that 'whatever is done among the right sort of people is right; and conversely, whatever is done among the wrong sort of people is wrong . . . [and] whatever can be done without unpleasant consequences is good.'[64] More specifically there is the cult of manliness. His father sends him to a public school which seems to be Pickthall's own school, Harrow. Before Limpidus enters school, his father gives him Polonius-like advice. Life at school will be rough at first, but it rubs the corners off a chap.

> 'A fellow who has not been through it is handicapped in life; especially one who has been brought up among women who give too much importance to religion, and all kinds of fads. You'll find out what is done by people of your sort, and learn to do it naturally. You'll learn to put religion, art, learning, and literature, and all such matters in their proper place, and not attach too much importance to 'em. At the same time you'll learn to tolerate a lot of things which your mother and your aunts, and women generally, condemn wholesale.'[65]

Women are for the amusement and solace of men but there are clear social and sexual frontiers. Plenty of girls exist to amuse the idle and the rich. They can be picked up and tossed aside. The aristocrat must avoid compromising himself and getting stung for breach of promise. But for the sake of marriage there are eligible brides, marriage with whom is like a treaty between families. As with Pickthall's accounts of marriage among upper-class Turks and Egyptians, love, affection and companionship are not to be assumed. For basically marriage is to preserve the property and name of the family, *his* family. Between the courtesan and the bride was a dangerous class of young lady, attractive and well-bred but unsuitable for either seduction or espousal. Such a one is the rector's daughter with whom the youthful Limpidus flirts until reprimanded by his worthy papa.

Limpidus' conventionality is impressive, so impressive that he becomes a man set apart from others. He rapidly acquires the slang and values of his school, of Cambridge and of Parliament. He gives a superbly conventional maiden speech and when he becomes a junior minister the permanent officials were

> fervent in their praise of his correct assumption of omniscience on their behalf, his bland refusal to concede the slightest information, the stern, reproachful air with which he crushed inquirers. He knew very little of the work of the department, but that did not matter. What the Government wanted was a man who could protect them from too close inquiries.[66]

Limpidus, in his youth, travels and here we see Pickthall in more familiar vein, observing the Englishman abroad. Limpidus travels with a friend of his father, an obsessive alpinist, Sir Barnet Veale. They are travelling by train through Normandy to Paris. Sir Barnet dozes over a newspaper. Limpidus ventures to comment:

> 'Good hunting country.'
> Sir Barnet looked round the edge of *The Times* and laughed:
> 'You should see 'em hunting. It would make you laugh. More like a minuet.'
> 'Don't they preserve at all? I can't see any coverts.'
> 'Only a few big landlords here and there.'
> Limpidus frowned and clicked his tongue despairingly.
> 'Wait till you see my mountains,' said Sir Barnet.[67]

The young man goes over the ground Pickthall knew so well but we meet no Egyptians, no Syrians, no Palestinians, no Turks. Egypt is a place where he shoots wild duck and quail, Palestine a place where he has 'a shot at wild boar in the Jordan valley; thence on to Asia Minor, where the sport was better.'[68]

We are in curiously familiar ground when Limpidus travels in Russia and becomes a Russophil. Pickthall, the fervent Russophobe, deals gently with Limpidus' sympathy for Russia's case against the Ottoman Empire. Limpidus' outlook fits in with a sentimental Liberal loyalty. A friendly and hospitable Russian prince persuades Limpidus that it was Disraeli who had set Britain against Russia. 'No doubt he was amused to set two Christian nations by the ears, to benefit the Musulman. A Jew and a Musulman is practically the same thing.'[69] But, the Russian goes on to say, 'I don't dislike the Turk. He has the manners of a gentleman. But he's a d....d unsociable fellow, for he doesn't drink.'[70] His host pours out more whisky and Limpidus agrees, adding solemnly: '"You and I are better. We're" – a hiccup – "Christians"'[71]

Sir Limpidus is a triumph of imagination over passion. We know that in the years before his novel was published, Pickthall saw a pro-Russian policy as a delusion that had dragged Europe into war. But without this knowledge we can accept the informed sincerity of Limpidus' own view of eastern politics. Limpidus is a credible creation. But when we know of Pickthall's championship of the Turks, of his conversion to Islam and his personal bitterness and fury about British foreign policy, *Sir Limpidus* turns into the blackest of black comedies. Those qualities displayed by Limpidus represent England at its worst: conformity to a collective public school ethos and adherence to a party line. They had led to a moral decline in the country. Six months before the publication of *Sir Limpidus*, Pickthall wrote that democracy was not to blame for this decline. 'The blame lies with the products of our public school and party discipline – men whose conscience has been broken so that they regard as natural in public business actions which would sicken a bargee.'[72] Pickthall's own social views had been coloured by the same conventions. But the year after the publication he turned his back on England, rejecting its social morality and politics in order to become as close to an Indian Muslim as it was possible for an Englishman to be.

NOTES TO INTRODUCTION

1. E.M. Forster, *Abinger Harvest* (Penguin Books, Harmondsworth, 1976 – but first published 1936), p.279

NOTES TO CHAPTER 1

1. In addition to Anne Fremantle, *Loyal Enemy* (Hutchinson, London, 1938), pp.5–16, the previous paragraphs are also based on G. Pickthall 'Chillesford' in Arthur Snell (ed.), *Handbook and Guide to the Parishes of Butley, Chillesford and Wantisden in the County of Suffolk* (The Wykeham Press, Winchester, n.d. (c. 1950)), pp.18–20; Roy Tricker, *St Peter's Church, Chillesford, Suffolk. History and Guide* (2nd edition) (Ipswich, 1983); church monuments at Broxbourne, Hertfordshire, and Chillesford Suffolk; interviews with Mrs Mary Snell, Chillesford, 20 September 1984 and with Dr Robert Pacey, Toynton All Saints, Lincolnshire, 15 June 1985; letters to the author from Mr William Hale, 28 March 1984, from Mrs Mary Snell, 27 September 1984, and Amanda J.E. Arrowsmith, County Archivist, Ipswich, 2 October 1984
2. D.C.M. Platt, *The Cinderella Service: British Consuls since 1825* (Longmans, London, 1971), p.166
3. *Oriental Encounters*, p.1
4. Ibid., p.2
5. Ibid., p.4
6. Ibid., p.5
7. Ibid., p.7
8. *Tales from Five Chimneys*, p.30
9. Fremantle, pp.81–2
10. *The Cultural Side of Islam*, p.37
11. *IRMI*, October 1919, VII, p.380
12. *IR*, February 1922, X, p.43
13. *NA*, 6 January 1916, XVIII, p.224
14. Fremantle, p.108
15. Ibid., p.110
16. *Athenaeum*, 1 August 1903, no 3953
17. *Critic*, May 1904, p.390
18. *Athenaeum*, 14 February 1914, no 4503, p.222
19. *NA*, 17 April 1919, XXIV, p.390
20. *IC*, January 1927, I, p.100
21. *NA*, 29 October 1914, XV, p.616
22. *NA*, 26 February 1914, XIV, p.520

23. J.E. Hanauer, *Folklore of the Holy Land* (Duckworth, London, 1907), p.xv
24. *Athenaeum*, 10 September 1910, no 4324, p.290
25. *Athenaeum*, 11 January 1913, no 4446, p.39
26. *NA*, 7 November 1912, XII, p.8
27. *The Nineteenth Century and After*, December 1912. LXXII, p.1142
28. *The Nineteenth Century and After*, December 1912, LXXII, p.1147
29. *NA*, 14 November 1912, XII, p.31
30. *Journal of the Central Asian Society*, April 1936, XXII, p.221
31. *NA*, 14 November 1912, XII, p.31
32. *NA*, 14 November 1912, XII, p.32

NOTES TO CHAPTER 2

1. *Athenaeum*, 16 May 1914, no 4516, p.678
2. *With the Turk in Wartime*, p.13
3. Ibid., p.35
4. Letter to Muriel Pickthall, 14 March 1913, in *IC*, July 1937, XI, p.421
5. *With the Turk in Wartime*, p.42
6. Ibid., p.211
7. *The Nineteenth Century and After*, September 1913, LXXIV, p.472
8. Feroz Ahmad, *The Young Turks* (Clarendon Press, Oxford, 1969), p.161
9. *With the Turk in Wartime*, p.43
10. Ibid., p.129
11. Ibid., p.136
12. Ibid., p.150
13. Ibid., p.151
14. Ibid., p.15
15. Letter to Muriel Pickthall, 26 March 1913, in *IC*, July 1937, XI, p.432
16. *With the Turk in Wartime*, p.106
17. Ibid., p.122
18. Ibid., p.198
19. Ibid., p.170
20. Ibid., p.216
21. *NA*, 12 November 1914, XVI, p.35
22. *NA*, 15 October 1914, XV, p.568
23. *NA*, 21 January 1915, XVI, p.305
24. *NA*, 15 October 1914, XV, p.568
25. *NA*, 27 August 1914, XV, p.392
26. *NA*, 27 August 1914, XV, p.392
27. *NA*, 15 October 1914, XV, pp.580–1
28. *NA*, 20 August 1914, XV, p.366
29. *Athenaeum*, 16 May 1914, no 4516, p.678
30. *NA*, 26 November 1914, XVI, p.90
31. *NA*, 31 December 1914, XVI, p.215
32. *NA*, 4 November 1915, XVIII, p.5
33. *NA*, 25 November 1915, XVIII, p.81. Toynbee seems to have been persuaded, in time, of the validity of the criticism, for in 1922 he referred to his own wartime anti-Turkish work as an example of western prejudice, 'of the wrong attitude towards the "Eastern Question"'. Arnold J. Toynbee, *The Western Question in Greece and Turkey* (Constable, London, 1922), p.382
34. H.F.V. Winstone, *The Illicit Adventure* (Jonathan Cape, London, 1982) p.434

35. Anne Fremantle, *Loyal Enemy* (Hutchinson, London, 1938), p.276
36. Christopher Sykes, *Two Studies in Virtue* (Collins, London, 1953), pp.207–8
37. *Friday Sermons*, p.43
38. *NA*, 3 February 1916, XVIII, p.334
39. *NA*, 8 October 1914, XV, p.544
40. *NA*, 12 November 1914, XVI, p.34
41. *NA*, 5 November 1914, XVI, p.9
42. *NA*, 10 December 1914, XVI, p.145
43. *IC*, April 1932, VI, p.326
44. *NA*, 19 June 1919, XXV, p.129
45. *IC*, April 1932, VI, p.326
46. *NA*, 20 August 1914, XV, 367. He had derived the notion of 'nose-cutting Serbs' from the account of an incident in *The Struggle for Scutari* by Mrs M. Edith Durham, which he reviewed on 20 June 1914 in the *Athenaeum*, no 4521, p.849
47. *NA*, 29 May 1919, XXV, p.91
48. *NA*, 11 March 1915, XVI, p.503

NOTES TO CHAPTER 3

1. *Friday Sermons*, p.16
2. Ibid., p.15
3. *NA*, 5 December 1912, XII, p.103
4. Anne Fremantle, *Loyal Enemy* (Hutchinson, London, 1938), p.105
5. Ibid., p.227
6. *IRMI*, January 1917, V, p.35
7. *ITMI*, January 1917, V, p.37
8. *IRMI*, January 1918, VI, p.4
9. The next few paragraphs are based primarily on early numbers of *Muslim India and the Islamic Review* and the typescript of a chapter of a forthcoming book on Islam in Britain by Mashouq Aly of the Islamic Foundation, Leicester, to whom I am much indebted.
10. *Muslim India and the Islamic Review*, January 1914, II, p.31
11. *IR*, April 1933, XXI, p.141
12. *IRMI*, April 1919, VII, p.122
13. *IRMI*, November 1919, VII, p.407
14. *Friday Sermons*, p.40
15. *IRMI*, November 1920, VIII, p.406
16. *IRMI*, December 1920, VIII, p.458
17. *IRMI*, December 1920, VIII, p.459
18. Fremantle, p.381
19. *Friday Sermons*, p.33
20. Ibid., p.5
21. *Friday Sermons*, p.5
22. *The Cultural Side of Islam*, p.101
23. *IRMI*, January 1918, VI, p.8
24. *Friday Sermons*, p.10
25. *The Cultural Side of Islam*, p.23
26. *IC*, January 1927, I, p.106
27. *NA*, 28 November 1912, XII, p.79
28. *IRMI*, January 1918, VI, p.7
29. *IC*, April 1935, IX, p.370

30. *IRMI*, February/March 1917, V, p.57
31. *IC*, April 1935, IX, p.368
32. *IC*, January 1937, XI, p.154
33. *The Cultural Side of Islam*, p.96
34. *IRMI*, April 1919, VII, p.131
35. *IRMI*, August 1918, VI, p.335
36. *IRMI*, May 1919, VII, p.174
37. *Islam and Progress*, p.28
38. *The Cultural Side of Islam*, p.125
39. Ibid., p.117
40. Ibid., p.192
41. *IRMI*, March 1919, VII, p.90
42. *IRMI*, March 1919, VII, p.94
43. *IRMI*, March 1919, VII, p.96
44. *The Cultural Side of Islam*, p.34
45. Ibid., p.35
46. A point made by Malise Ruthven, *Islam in the World* (Penguin Books, Harmondsworth, 1984), pp.165–6
47. *Islam and Progress*, p.13
48. Ibid., p.18
49. *The Cultural Side of Islam*, p.138
50. Ibid., pp.138–9
51. Ibid., p.135
52. *IRMI*, December 1919, VII, p.441
53. *IRMI*, December 1919, VII, p.444
54. *IRMI*, October 1919, VII, p.380
55. *IRMI*, April 1919, VII, p.143
56. *IRMI*, April 1919, VII, p.145
57. *IRMI*, April 1919, VII, p.146
58. *IRMI*, April 1919, VII, p.148
59. *IRMI*, March 1917, V, p.59
60. *IRMI*, July 1918, VI, p.286
61. *Friday Sermons*, p.2
62. Ibid., pp.42–3
63. *Islam and Progress*, p.66
64. Ibid., p.33
65. *The Cultural Side of Islam*, p.129
66. *IRMI*, May 1919, VII, p.180
67. *The Cultural Side of Islam*, p.63
68. Iibid., p.121
69. *IRMI*, May 1919, VII, p.172
70. *IC*, July 1927, I, p.490
71. *IC*, July 1927, I, p.496
72. *IC*, July 1927, I, p.497
73. *IC*, July 1927, III, p.481
74. *IRMI*, May 1919, VII, p.181

NOTES TO CHAPTER 4

1. Anne Fremantle, *Loyal Enemy* (Hutchinson, London, 1938), p.407

Notes

2. Bernard Lewis, *The Emergence of Modern Turkey* (Oxford University Press, 1961), p.317
3. Lewis, p.318
4. Valentine Chirol, *Fifty Years in a Changing World* (Jonathan Cape, London, 1927), p.90
5. Afzal Iqbal, *The Life and Times of Mohamed Ali* (Institute of Islamic Culture, Lahore, 1974), p.15
6. P.C. Bamford, *Histories of the Non Cooperation and Khilafat Movements* (Government of India Press, Delhi, 1925), p.145
7. Iqbal, p.217
8. Fremantle, p.330
9. *IR*, January 1921, IX, p.15
10. Fremantle, p.332
11. Iqbal, p.291
12. Fremantle, p.374
13. *Cornhill Magazine*, September 1924, LVII, p.368
14. *Cornhill Magazine*, June 1926, LX, p.690
15. *IR*, November 1923, XI, p.391
16. *Journal of the Central Asian Society*, April 1936, XXII, p.227
17. *IR*, December 1924, XII, p.433
18. *IR*, December 1924, XII, p.432
19. *Geographical Magazine*, April 1936, no 6, p.400
20. *IC*, April 1931, V, p.337
21. *IC*, July 1928, II, p. 466
22. *IC*, July 1928, II, pp.464–71
23. Mohammad Shafiuddin to the author, 29 November 1983
24. Hameeduddin Ahmed to the author, 13 February 1984
25. *IC*, July 1936, X, p.499
26. *IC*, January 1936, X, pp.164–5
27. *IC*, July 1931, V, p.683
28. *Journal of the Central Asian Society*, April 1936, XXII, p.230
29. *IRMI*, January 1919, VII, p.11
30. *The Glorious Koran*, p.vi
31. *Athenaeum*, 27 February 1915, no 4557, p.184
32. *IRMI*, February-March 1917, V, p.55
33. *The Glorious Koran*, p.705n
34. *IRMI*, January 1919, VII, p.16
35. Fremantle, p.389
36. *IC*, July 1931, V, p.423
37. *IC*, July 1931, V, p.427
38. *IC*, July 1931, V, p.425
39. Elie Kedourie, *The Chatham House Version and other Middle-Eastern Studies* (Weidenfeld and Nicolson, London, 1970), p.183
40. Jacques Berque, *l'Egypte. Impérialisme et Révolution* (Gallimard, Paris, 1967), p.286
41. *IC*, July 1931, V, p.427
42. *IC*, July 1931, V, pp.432–3
43. *IC*, July 1931, V, p.433
44. I am grateful for help on this controversy from Dr R.C. Ostle of the School of Oriental and African Studies, University of London. See also A.J. Arberry, *The Seven Odes* (Allen and Unwin, London, 1957), pp.228–30, 238; and Albert Hourani, *Arabic Thought in the Liberal Age 1798–1939* (Oxford University Press, 1962), p.327
45. *IC*, July 1930, IV, pp.481–2
46. *IC*, January 1934, VIII, p.152

47. I am indebted to Professor Muhammad Hamidullah of Paris for help in tracing these Turkish translations

48. Information kindly provided by Mr Rayner Unwin of Allen and Unwin

49. Fremantle, p.389

50. Muhammad Asad to the author, 8 August 1984

51. Hameeduddin Ahmed to the author, 2 February 1984

52. *Dawn*, 9 April 1982

53. *Dawn*, 19 April 1982

54. Hameeduddin Ahmed to the author, 2 February 1984. See also S. Sakhawat Ali, 'Some Mistakes in Pickthall's "Translation of the Holy Quran"', *Minaret*, November 1983, pp.19–23

55. Anand G. Chandavarkar to the author, 29 August 1983

56. *Friday Sermons*, p.27

57. *IC*, January 1937, XI, p.1

NOTES TO CHAPTER 5

1. *As Others See Us*, pp.71–85

2. *Pot au Feu*, pp.305–21

3. Ibid., p.352

4. Ibid., p.356

5. *Tales from Five Chimneys*, p.121

6. *As Other See Us*, pp.154–70

7. Ibid., pp.103–19

8. *Pot au Feu*, pp.271–88

9. Ibid., p.275

10. *Tales from Five Chimneys*, p.157

11. Ibid., p.56

12. *As Others See Us*, p.49

13. Ibid., pp.69–70

14. *Tales from Five Chimneys*, p.130

15. *As Others See Us*, p.2

16. Ibid., pp.7–8

17. Ibid., p.8

18. *Pot au Feu*, pp.289–304

19. Ibid., p.290

20. Ibid., p.293

21. Ibid., pp.298–9

22. Ibid., p.299

23. Ibid., p.302

24. For a historical account of these events, see Moshe Ma'oz, *Ottoman Reform in Syria and Palestine 1840–1861* (Clarendon Press, Oxford, 1968), pp.231–40 and Linda Schatkowski Schilcher, *Families in Politics* (Franz Steiner, Stuttgart, 1985), pp.87–100

25. *Saïd the Fisherman*, p.39

26. Ibid., pp.217–18

27. Ibid., p.191

28. Ibid., p.64

29. Ibid., p.65

30. Ibid., p.52

31. Ibid., p.53

32. Ibid., p.2
33. Ibid., p.97
34. Ibid., p.122
35. Ibid., p.134
36. Ibid., p.261
37. For example, W.H.T. Gairdner, *The Reproach of Islam* (The Church of Scotland, Edinburgh, 1909), pp.138–9. Pickthall's novel is cited as evidence to support the view
38. *Saïd the Fisherman*, p.165
39. *The House of Islam*, p.82
40. Ibid., p.139
41. Ibid., p.141
42. Ibid., p.237
43. Ibid., p.97
44. Ibid., p.228
45. *The Myopes*, p.96
46. *The Children of the Nile*, p.206
47. Ibid., p.202
48. Ibid., p.203
49. Ibid., p.149
50. Ibid., p.223
51. Ibid., p.141
52. Ibid., pp.8–9
53. Ibid., p.33
54. Ibid., p.14
55. Ibid., pp.307–8
56. Ibid., p.314
57. Ibid., p.316
58. Ibid., p.175
59. *The Valley of the Kings*, p.175
60. Ibid., pp.58–9
61. Ibid., p.23
62. Ibid., p.320
63. Ibid., p.61
64. Ibid., p.265
65. Ibid., p.321
66. Ibid., p.271
67. Ibid., p.285
68. Ibid., p.339
69. Ibid., p.18
70. Ibid., p.327
71. Ibid., p.265. Compare Derek Hopwood – *The Russian Presence in Syria and Palestine 1843–1914* (The Clarendon Press, Oxford, 1969), pp.199–200
72. Ibid., p.332
73. *Veiled Women*, p.108
74. Ibid., p.110
75. Ibid., p.116
76. Ibid., p.148
77. Ibid., p.154
78. Ibid., p.223
79. Ibid., p.224
80. Ibid., p.123
81. Ibid., p.124

82. Ibid., p.171
83. Ibid., p.171–3. E.M. Forster in his essay praising Pickthall's work also praises *Le Livre de Goha le Simple* by Albert Adès and Albert Josipovici, Calmann-Levy, Paris, 1919. This novel also has a brief account of a zar – there called tar, p.247
84. *Veiled Women*, p.65
85. Ibid., p.248
86. Ibid., p.249
87. Ibid., p.255
88. Ibid., p.269
89. Ibid., p.51
90. Ibid., p.265
91. *The House of War*, p.v
92. Ibid., p.104
93. Ibid., p.138
94. Ibid., p.27
95. Ibid., p.263
96. Ibid., p.27
97. Ibid., p.317
98. *Knights of Araby*, Foreword
99. IC, July 1931, V, p.496
100. *The Cultural Side of Islam*, p.80
101. Henry Cassels Kay (editor and translator), *Yaman, Its Early Mediaeval History* (Rivingtons, London, 1892; reprinted Gregg, London, 1968)
102. Kay, p.34
103. *Knights of Araby*, p.175
104. Ibid., p.183
105. Kay, p.35
106. *Knights of Araby*, p.47
107. Ibid., p.48
108. Ibid., pp.13–14
109. Ibid., p.197
110. *The Cultural Side of Islam*, p.40
111. *Knights of Araby*, p.232
112. Ibid., pp.380–1
113. *Oriental Encounters*, p.9
114. Ibid., p.17
115. Ibid., p.273
116. Ibid., p.38
117. Ibid., p.67
118. For example, the story of Joha and the tent-peg, *Oriental Encounters*, p.251, Hanauer, p.85; and the custom that it was licit to pick fruit at the edge of an orchard, *Oriental Encounters*, p.283, Hanauer, p.116. Pickthall also alludes to this practice in *Saïd the Fisherman*, p.228
119. *Oriental Encounters*, p.94
120. Ibid., pp.100–1
121. Ibid., p.267
122. Ibid., p.98
123. Ibid., p.211
124. Ibid., p.216
125. Ibid., p.77
126. Ibid., pp.45–6
127. Ibid., p.109
128. Ibid., p.184

129. *The Early Hours*, p.269
130. Ibid., p.9
131. Ibid., p.120
132. Ibid., p.217
133. Bernard Lewis, *The Emergence of Modern Turkey* (Oxford University Press, 1961), p.223
134. *NA*, 26 November 1914, XVI, p.90
135. *The Early Hours*, p.103
136. Ibid., p.104. Another example: The Minister of War, Nazim Pasha, who was killed in January 1913 was reputed to be a heavy drinker. Pickthall had in his possession a Turkish comic paper of the Unionist party 'with a picture of Nazim Pasha in a state of jovial intoxication, a whiskey-bottle half out of his pocket . . . asking at a booking office for a circular ticket for Sofia, Belgrade, Athens, and Cettinje, durable one month'. (*NA*, 24 December 1914, XVI, p.191). The cartoon illustrated the unbounded optimism of the Minister in his expectations of the outcome of the war with Bulgaria, Serbia, Greece and Albania. The cartoon is described in virtually the same words in *The Early Hours*, p.238
137. *The Early Hours*, pp.170–1. Compare *With the Turk in Wartime*, p.42 and p.211
138. Ibid., pp.45–6
139. Ibid., pp.215–16

NOTES TO CHAPTER 6

1. *Athenaeum*, 2 July 1910, no 4314, p.8
2. *Tales from Five Chimneys*, pp.286–7
3. *Pot au Feu*, p.197
4. Ibid., p.110
5. G. Pickthall (Pickthall's half-sister, Grace) – 'Chillesford' in Arthur Snell (ed.), *Handbook and Guide to the Parishes of Butley, Chillesford and Wantisden in the County of Suffolk* (The Wykeham Press, Winchester, n.d. (c.1950)), p.19
6. *Pot au Feu*, p.41
7. Ibid., p.50
8. Ibid., p.50; *Tales from Five Chimneys*, p.273; and elsewhere
9. *Tales from Five Chimneys*, p.217. Another of his half-sisters, Caroline, also interested herself in Suffolk dialect, publishing a few dialect tales and poems and a glossary of East Suffolk words. See Carol Christie (sc. Caroline Pickthall), *Walberswick Notes* (St Catherine Press, London, 1911)
10. *As Others See Us*,
11. Ibid., p.261
12. Ibid., p.271
13. Ibid., p.272
14. Ibid., p.272
15. Ibid., pp.273–4
16. Ibid., p.274
17. Ibid., p.275
18. *All Fools*, p.28
19. Ibid., p.222
20. Ibid., p.50
21. Ibid., p.55
22. Ibid., p.245
23. Ibid., p.129

24. *Enid*, p.110
25. Ibid., p.338
26. Ibid., p.121
27. Ibid., p.121
28. Ibid., p.209
29. Ibid., p.147
30. Ibid., p.84
31. Ibid., p.10
32. *Brendle*, p.241. Another half-sister, Ethel, studied at the London School of Art in 1888
33. Ibid., p.155
34. Ibid., p.44
35. Ibid., p.61
36. Ibid., p.109
37. Ibid., p.4
38. Ibid., p.237
39. Ibid., p.236
40. Ibid., p.186
41. Ibid., p.192
42. *The Myopes*, p.2
43. Ibid., p.291
44. Ibid., p.24
45. Ibid., p.282
46. Ibid., p.148
47. Ibid., p.47
48. Ibid., p.195
49. Ibid., p.291
50. *Larkmeadow*, p.24
51. Ibid., p.109
52. *The Cultural Side of Islam*, p.144
53. *Larkmeadow*, p.325
54. Ibid., p.288
55. Ibid., p.93
56. *NA*, June 1915, XVII, p.103
57. *Larkmeadow*, p.62
58. Ibid., p.7
59. Ibid., p.149
60. *Athenaeum*, 2 July 1910, no 4314, p.8. This appears in a review of a history of Theberton, the Suffolk home of Charles Montagu Doughty. The history is by Doughty's brother, Henry
61. *Sir Limpidus*, p.80
62. Ibid., p.94
63. Ibid., pp.144–5
64. Ibid., pp.38–9
65. Ibid., p.17
66. Ibid., p.191
67. Ibid., p.110
68. Ibid., p.123
69. Ibid., p.127
70. Ibid., pp.127–8
71. Ibid., p.128
72. *NA*, 12 June 1919, XXV, p.112

A MARMADUKE
PICKTHALL
BIBLIOGRAPHY

What follows is an interim chronological bibliography. I have traced books, pamphlets, articles, reviews and letters Pickthall published in England. He wrote for a wide range of periodicals and I am sure much has been missed. Similarly I am aware of the incompleteness of the record of publications in India – articles in the *Bombay Chronicle* and ephemeral publications elsewhere. I therefore head this section with the indefinite article in the hope that another will take over where I have left off and produce *the* Pickthall bibliography.

1898

1. January. (E. Greck) – 'Monsieur le President', *Temple Bar*, CXIII, pp.55–63; reprinted in *Pot au Feu* (1911), pp.215–30
2. July. (E. Greck) – 'The Word of an Englishman', *Temple Bar*, CXIII, pp.365–74; reprinted in *Littell's Living Age*, August, CCXVIII, pp.396–402, reprinted in *Tales from Five Chimneys* (1915), pp.1–16

1899

1. January. 'A Question of Precedence', *Temple Bar*, CXIV, pp.76–81; reprinted in *Pot au Feu* (1911), pp.263–70

1900

1. March. *All Fools*, Swan and Sonnenschein, London

Marmaduke Pickthall

1903

1. July. *Saïd the Fisherman*, Methuen and Co., London; McClure Phillips, New York; republished by A.A. Knopf, New York, 1923; Blue Jade Library, New York, 1925; republished with an introduction and additional notes by Peter Clark, Quartet Books, London, 1986

1904

1. June. *Enid*, Archibald Constable and Company, Westminster

1905

1. September. *Brendle*, Methuen and Co., London; republished by W. Collins, London, 1909
2. December. 'Mauvaises Herbes de l'Ame', *Temple Bar*, CXXXII, pp.549–70

1906

1. September. *The House of Islam*, Methuen and Co., London; D. Appleton and Co., New York

1907

1. Introduction to J.E. Hanauer – *Folklore of the Holy Land: Moslem, Christian, and Jewish*, Duckworth, London, pp.xi–xix
2. November. *The Myopes*, John Murray, London

1908

1. August. 'Found in an Old Bureau', *Blackwood's Magazine*, CLXXXIV, pp.258–66; reprinted in *Pot au Feu* (1911), pp.146–60
2. September. *The Children of the Nile*, John Murray, London; republished by Thomas Nelson, Edinburgh and London, 1917

1909

1. 28 August. Unsigned review of *The White Prophet* by Hall Caine, *Athenaeum*, no. 4270, p.232
2. 11 September. Unsigned review of *The Punishment* by Thomas McKean, *Athenaeum*, no. 4272, p.293
3. 2 October. Unsigned review of *In Ambush* by Marie von Horst, *Athenaeum*, no. 4275, p.389
4. 16 October. Unsigned review of *Things Seen in Egypt* by E.L. Butcher, *Athenaeum*, no. 4277, p.460
5. November. *The Valley of the Kings*, John Murray, London; republished by A.A. Knopf, New York, 1913; and by J.M. Dent, London, 1914
6. 6 November. Unsigned review of *The Tenants of Pixy Farm* by Maude Goldring, *Athenaeum*, no. 4280, p.554
7. 6 November. Unsigned review of *The Desert Dreamers* by Kathlyn Rhodes, *Athenaeum*, no. 4280, p.554
8. 4 December. Unsigned review of *Going Down to Jerusalem* by Norman Duncan, *Athenaeum*, no. 4284, p.694

A Pickthall Bibliography

1910

1. April. 'Karàkter', *Cornhill Magazine*, XXVIII, pp.525–34; reprinted in *Littell's Living Age*, 7 May, CCLXV, pp.362–9, reprinted in *Pot au Feu* (1911), pp.289–304
2. 21 May. Unsigned review of *Modern Arabic Stories, Ballads, Proverbs, and Idioms* collected by A.O. Green, *Athenaeum*, no. 4308, p.605
3. 30 June. 'The Situation in Egypt, a Reply to Duse Mohamed', *NA*, VII, p.196
4. 2 July. Unsigned review of *Chronicles of Theberton* by Henry Montagu Doughty, *Athenaeum*, no. 4314, p.8
5. 23 July. Unsigned review of *Diana of Dreams* by G.B. Burgin, *Athenaeum*, no. 4317, p.93
6. 10 September. Unsigned review of *Allah the Avenger* by F. Cowley Whitehouse, *Athenaeum*, no. 4324, p.290
7. 10 September. Unsigned review of *Did Cupid Count?* by M. Knight, *Athenaeum*, no. 4324, p.290
8. 17 September. Unsigned review of *The Holy Bible*, *Athenaeum*, no. 4324, p.332
9. 8 October. Unsigned review of *The Incubus* by Helen Hester Colvill, *Athenaeum*, no. 4328, p.416
10. 8 October. Unsigned review of *Separate Stars* by Violet Pearn, *Athenaeum*, no. 4328, p.416
11. 29 October. Unsigned review of *Seed of Fire*, by Rachel Swete Macnamara, *Athenaeum*, no. 4331, p.518
12. 3 December. Unsigned review of *The Holy Land* by Robert Hichens, *Athenaeum*, no. 4336, p.694
13. 3 December. Unsigned review of *The Gates: A Study in Prose*, *Athenaeum*, no. 4336, p.701
14. 17 December. Unsigned review of *The Parables*, illustrated by Eugene Burnard, *Athenaeum*, no. 4338, p.740

1911

1. February. 'Tale of a Camp', *Cornhill Magazine*, XXX, pp.213–22; reprinted in *Pot au Feu*, pp.336–51
2. February. *Pot au Feu*, John Murray, London
3. 11 February. Unsigned review of Macmillan's *Guide to Palestine and Syria*, *Athenaeum*, no. 4346, p.157
4. 11 February. Unsigned review of *The Church of Nativity at Bethlehem* by W. Harvey, W.R. Lethaby and others, *Athenaeum*, no. 4346, p.168
5. 11 March. Unsigned review of *The Unseen Barrier*, by Morice Gerard, *Athenaeum*, no. 4350, p.273
6. 11 March. Unsigned review of *The Downsman* by Maude Goldring, *Athenaeum*, no. 4350, p.273
7. 6 May. Unsigned review of *Sinai in Spring* by M.J. Rendall, *Athenaeum*, no. 4358, pp.506–7
8. 27 May. Unsigned review of *The General Plan* by Edmund Candler, *Athenaeum*, no. 4361, p.600
9. 10 June. Unsigned review of *A Bird in the Hand* by Rosalind Devis–Browne, *Athenaeum*, no. 4364, p.656
10. 12 August. Unsigned review of *Mrs Drummond's Vocation* by Mark Ryce, *Athenaeum*, no. 4372, p.181
11. 9 September. Unsigned review of *The Earthen Drum* by E.S. Stevens, *Athenaeum*, no. 4376, p.296

Marmaduke Pickthall

12. 4 November. Unsigned review of *The Verge of Twilight* by E.O. Carolin, *Athenaeum*, no. 4384, pp.552–3
13. 18 November. Unsigned review of *Studies in Galilee* by Ernest W. Gurney, *Athenaeum*, no. 4386, p.624
14. 23 December. Unsigned review of *A Journalist in the Holy Land* by Arthur E. Copping, *Athenaeum*, no. 4391, p.792
15. 23 December. Unsigned review of *Palestine* by G.E. Franklin, *Athenaeum*, no. 4391, p.792

1912

1. August. *Larkmeadow*, Chatto and Windus, London
2. November. 'His Honour's Pleasure', *Cornhill Magazine*, XXXIII, pp.672–83; reprinted in *Littell's Living Age*, 28 December, CCLXXV, pp.800–8; reprinted in *Tales from Five Chimneys* (1915), pp.120–37
3. November. Unsigned review of *Scenes in the Life of Nazareth* by William Hole, *Athenaeum*, no. 4436, p.529
4. 7 November. 'The Black Crusade', Part 1, *NA*, XII, p.8
5. 14 November. 'The Black Crusade', Part 2, *NA*, XII, pp.31–2
6. 21 November. 'The Black Crusade', Part 3, *NA*, XII, p.58
7. 28 November. 'The Black Crusade', Part 4, 'The Victims', *NA*, XII, p.79
8. 28 November. 'The Black Crusade', (letter), *NA*, XII, p.93
9. December. 'Outlook in the Near East: For El Islam', *The Nineteenth Century and After*, LXXII, pp.1141–9; reprinted in *Littell's Living Age*, 18 January 1913, CCLXXVI, pp.131–7
10. 5 December. 'The Black Crusade', Part 5, *NA*. XII, p.103
11. 26 December. 'The Future of Islam', *NA*, XII, pp.175–6
12. 28 December. Unsigned review of *Travel Pictures* by Bhawani Singh and of *The Land that is Desolate* by Frederick Treves, *Athenaeum*, no. 4444, p.777

1913

1. *The Black Crusade* (reprint of items 4–7 and 10, 1913), The New Age Press, London
2. January. *Veiled Women*, Eveleigh Nash, London; Duffield and Co., New York
3. 9 January. 'Our Fellow Christians' (letter), *NA*, XII, p.238
4. 11 January. Unsigned review of *Eothen* by A.W. Kinglake, *Athenaeum*, no. 4446, p.39
5. 18 January. 'A Protest' (letter about massacres of Muslims in Macedonia), *The Times*
6. 8 February. Unsigned review of *Djelal, Histoire Turque* by Jean Marsol, *Athenaeum*, no. 4450, p.164
7. 8 February. Unsigned note on anonymous reviews, *Athenaeum*, no. 4450, p.164
8. 8 February. Unsigned review of *A Camera Crusade through the Holy Land* by Dwight L. Elmendorf, *Athenaeum*, no. 4450, p.168
9. 20 February. 'The Fate of the Mohammedans of Macedonia' (letter), *NA*, XII, pp.388–9
10. 22 February. Unsigned review of *La Vie Compliquée* by Fernand Nicolay, *Athenaeum*, no. 4452, p.221
11. 1 March. Unsigned review of *The Immoveable East* by Philip J. Baldensperger, *Athenaeum*, no. 4453, p.242
12. 15 May. 'Balkan Atrocities' (letter), *NA*. XIII, pp.68–9
13. 9 August. Unsigned review of *The Ottoman Empire 1801–1913* by William Miller, *Athenaeum*, no. 4476, pp.129–30

14. 16 August. Unsigned review of *Fin de Turquie* by Claude Farrère, *Athenaeum*, no. 4477, pp.150–1

15. September. 'The Hope of Moslem Progress', *The Nineteenth Century and After*, LXXIV, pp.472–9

16. 11 September. 'A Pilgrimage to Turkey During War Time', Part 1, *NA*, XIII, pp.566–7

17. 18 September. 'A Pilgrimage to Turkey During War Time', Part 2, 'Stamboul and Pera', XIII, pp.594–5

18. 20 September. Unsigned review of *The Broken Halo* by Florence L. Barclay, *Athenaeum*, no. 4482, p.276

19. 25 September. 'A Pilgrimage to Turkey During War Time', Part 3, 'House Hunting', *NA*, XIII, pp.629–30

20. 27 September. Unsigned review of *The Woman Flinches* by Mrs Fred Reynolds, *Athenaeum*, no. 4483, p.315

21. 2 October. 'A Pilgrimage to Turkey During War Time', Part 4, 'Pinetree Kiosk', *NA*, XIII, pp.657–8

22. 9 October. 'A Pilgrimage to Turkey During War Time', Part 5, 'The Neighbours', *NA*, XIII, pp.691–2

23. 16 October. 'A Pilgrimage to Turkey During War Time', Part 6, 'Views of England', *NA*, XIII, pp.723–4

24. 23 October. 'A Pilgrimage to Turkey During War Time', Part 7, 'A Garden-Party', *NA*, XIII, pp.753–5

25. 30 October. 'A Pilgrimage to Turkey During War Time', Part 8, 'A Modern Khoja', *NA*, XIII, pp.788–9

26. 6 November. 'A Pilgrimage to Turkey During War Time', Part 9, 'Ottoman Greeks', *NA*, XIV, pp.11–12

27. 8 November. Unsigned review of *The Banks of the Nile* by Ella Du Cane, *Athenaeum*, no. 4489, p.532

28. 13 November. 'A Pilgrimage to Turkey During War Time', Part 10, 'The Woman Question', *NA*, XIV, pp.44–6

29. 20 November. 'A Pilgrimage to Turkey During War Time', Part 11, 'Political Gossip', *NA*, XIV, pp.75–6

30. 21 November. 'The Ethics of Aristotle' (letter), *The Near East*, p.75

31. 27 November. 'A Pilgrimage to Turkey During War Time', Part 12, 'A Conspirator', *NA*, XIV, pp.110–11

32. 27 November. 'A Plea for Civilisation' (letter), *NA*, XIV, p.124

33. 4 December. 'A Pilgrimage to Turkey During War Time', Part 13, 'Eleventh of June', *NA*, XIV, pp.141–2

34. 11 December. 'A Pilgrimage to Turkey During War Time', Part 14, 'Assassination a Tonic', *NA*, XIV, pp.172–3

35. 11 December. 'England and Turkey' (letter), *NA*, XIV, p.189

36. 18 December. 'A Pilgrimage to Turkey During War Time', Part 15, 'The End and Cause of the Conspiracy', *NA*, XIV, pp.202–4

37. 19 December. 'The Ethics of Aristotle' (letter), *The Near East*, p.233

38. 25 December. 'A Pilgrimage to Turkey During War Time', Part 16, 'The Army of the West', *NA*, XIV, pp.233–4

1914

1. 1 January. 'A Pilgrimage to Turkey During War Time', Part 17, 'Ottoman vs. Cosmopolitan Education', *NA*, XIV, pp.266–8

2. 8 January. 'A Pilgrimage to Turkey During War Time', Part 18, 'Checks on Progress', *NA*, XIV, pp.301–2

3. 15 January. 'A Pilgrimage to Turkey During War Time', Part 19, 'Islam and Progress', *NA*, XIV, pp.333–4

4. 7 February. Unsigned review of *Black Ivory and White, or The Story of El Zubeir Pasha*, *Athenaeum*, no. 4502, p.195

5. 14 February. Unsigned review of *Egypt in Transition* by Sidney Low, *Athenaeum*, no. 4503, p.222

6. 26 February. 'Concerning Denshawai', *NA*, XIV, pp.519–20

7. March. *With the Turk in Wartime* (reprint of 'A Pilgrimage to Turkey During War Time', items 16–17, 19, 21–26, 28–29, 31, 33–34, 36; 38, 1913; 1–3, 1914), J.M. Dent, London

8. 12 March. 'Denshawai and After' (letter), *NA*, XIV, pp.603–4

9. 14 March. Unsigned review of *The Last English* by George Bertram, *Athenaeum*, no. 4507, p.177

10. 26 March. 'The Turkish Parties', *NA*, XIV, pp.668–9

11. 18 April. Unsigned review of *The New Tripoli* by Ethel Braun, *Athenaeum*, no. 4512, pp.548–9

12. 16 May. Unsigned review of *Turkish Memories* by Sidney Whitman, *Athenaeum*, no. 4516, pp.677–8

13. 16 May. Unsigned note on Arabic words, *Athenaeum*, no. 4516, p.689

14. 23 May. Unsigned review of *Vagabonds in Perigord* by H.H. Bashford, *Athenaeum*, no. 4517, p.689

15. 30 May. Unsigned review of *The Inner History of the Balkan War*, by Reginald Rankin, *Athenaeum*, no. 4518, p.713

16. 20 June. Unsigned review of *The Struggle for Scutari* by M. Edith Durham and *The Orient Express* by Arthur Moores, *Athenaeum*, no. 4521, p.849

17. 11 July. Unsigned review of *The Women of Egypt* by Elizabeth Cooper, *Athenaeum*, no. 4524, p.45

18. 15 August. Unsigned review of *A Child of the Orient* by Demetra Vaka, *Athenaeum*, no. 4529, p.193

19. 20 August. 'Teuton and Slav: a Word in Season', *NA*, XV, pp.366–7

20. 27 August. 'The Head of the Triple Entente', *NA*, XV, p.392

21. 29 August. Unsigned review of *Travel and Politics in Armenia* by Noel and Harold Buxton, *Athenaeum*, no. 4531, p.230

22. 3 September. 'Turkey and the European War', *NA*, XV, p.417

23. 10 September. 'Friends and Countrymen', *NA*, XV, pp.440–1

24. 17 September. 'Rustic War-notes' (letter), *NA*, XV, p.485

25. 24 September. 'Turkish Independence', Part 1, *NA*, XV, p.500

26. 1 October. 'Turkish Independence', Part 2, *NA*, XV, p.520

27. 8 October. 'Turkish Independence', Part 3, *NA*, XV, pp.543–4

28. 15 October. 'Turkish Independence', Part 4, *NA*, XV, pp.568–9

29. 15 October. 'Turkish Independence' (letter), *NA*, XV, pp.580–1

30. 22 October. 'Turkish Independence', Part 5, *NA*, XV, pp.592–3

31. 29 October. 'Egypt and the Foreign Office', *NA*, XV, p.616

32. 29 October. 'Turkey and Mr Pickthall' (letter), *NA*, XV, p.631

33. 5 November. 'The Arab Question', *NA*, XVI, p.9

34. 5 November. 'Turkish Independence' (letter), *NA*, XVI, p.29

35. 12 November. 'Turkish Independence', *NA*, XVI, pp.34–5

36. 12 November. 'Turkish Independence', *NA*, XVI, pp.47–8

37. 19 November. 'What Next!' *NA*, XVI, pp.63–4

38. 26 November. 'Six Years', Part 1, *NA*, XVI, pp.90–1

39. 3 December. 'Six Years', Part 2, *NA*, XVI, p.119

40. 10 December. 'Six Years', Part 3, *NA*, XVI, pp.144–5

41. 17 December. 'Six Years', Part 4, *NA*, XVI, p.168

42. 24 December. 'Six Years', Part 5, *NA*, XVI, p.191
43. 31 December. 'Six years', Part 6, *NA*, XVI, pp.214–15

1915

1. 7 January. 'The Case of Egypt', *NA*, XVI, p.240
2. 14 January. 'Sultan of Egypt', *NA*, XVI, pp.272–3
3. 14 January. 'The Turkish Point of View' (letter), *NA*, XVI, pp.290–2
4. 21 January. 'Pan Islamism as a British Policy', *NA*, XVI, pp.304–5
5. 28 January. 'After the Caliphate', *NA*, XVI, pp.336–7
6. 4 February. 'The Russian Policy', *NA*, XVI, p.368
7. 11 February. 'National Honour and Personal Honour', *NA*, XVI, p.399
8. 13 February. Unsigned review of *A Pilgrim's Scrip* by R. Campbell Thompson, *Athenaeum*, no. 4555, p.136
9. 18 February. 'The Project of Partition', *NA*, XVI, p.424
10. 25 February. 'A Troublesome Neighbour', *NA*, XVI, p.449
11. 27 February. Unsigned review of *An Englishwoman in a Turkish Harem* by Grace Ellison, *Athenaeum*, no. 4557, p.184
12. 11 March. 'The Fate of Turkey', *NA*, XVI, p.503
13. 11 March. 'Foreign Affairs' (letter), *NA*, XVI, p.516
14. 18 March. 'A Friend of Progress' (letter), *NA*, XVI, pp. 546–8
15. 25 March. 'Nature and the Doctrinaire', *NA*, XVI, pp.559–60
16. 1 April. 'Commercialism and Politics' (letter), *NA*. XVI, pp.596–7
17. 1 May. Unsigned review of *The Record of Nicholas Freydon: An Autobiography*, *Athenaeum*, no. 4566, p.400
18. 13 May. 'Turkey and Egypt' (letter), *NA*, XVII, pp.45–6
19. June. *Tales from Five Chimneys*, Mills and Boon, London
20. 3 June. 'Oriental Local Government', *NA*, XVII, pp.103–4
21. 24 June. 'Foreign Affairs etc' (letter), *NA*, XVII, p.189
22. 8 July. 'Foreign Affairs' (letter), *NA*, XVII, pp.237–8
23. 14 October. 'Letters from Russia' (letter), *NA*, XVII, p.581
24. 21 October. 'In Defence of British Diplomacy', *NA*, XVII, pp.590–1
25. 28 October. 'On the Coaxing of Neutrals', *NA*, XVII, p.613
26. 4 November. '"Defence of the Realm" in Turkey', *NA*, XVIII, pp.5–6
27. 11 November. 'Servia or Constantinople', *NA*, XVIII, p.33
28. 18 November. 'While Europe Fought', *NA*, XVIII, pp.56–7
29. 25 November. 'The Gospel of Hate', *NA*, XVIII, pp.80–1
30. 2 December. 'In Memory of British Statesmanship', *NA*, XVIII, pp.102–3
31. 9 December. 'The Survival of the Fittest', *NA*, XVIII, pp.127–8
32. 9 December. 'The Armenian Massacres' (letter), *NA*, XVIII, p.142
33. 16 December. 'Armenian Atrocities', *NA*, XVIII, pp.153–5
34. 23 December. 'England in the East', *NA*, XVIII, pp.176–7
35. 30 December. 'Egypt and the Canal', *NA*, XVIII, p.202

1916

1. 6 January. 'The Last Chance', *NA*, XVIII, pp.223–4
2. February. *The House of War*, Eveleigh Nash, London; Duffield and Co., New York
3. 3 February. 'Turkey and England' (letter), *NA*, XVIII, pp.333–4
4. 30 March. 'The Cloud in the Far East', *NA*, XVIII, pp.510–11
5. 30 April. 'Moslem Civilization after the War', *New York Times*
6. 4 May. 'Sir Mark Sykes and the Armenians', *NA*, XIX, p.6
7. 4 May. 'The Aga Khan' (letter), *NA*, XIX, pp.20–1

8. 6 July. 'Islam and Progress', Part 1, 'The Priesthood of the Human Mind', *NA*, XIX, pp.225–6

9. 13 July. 'Islam and Progress', Part 2, 'The Position of Women' and Part 3, 'Fatalism', *NA*, XIX, pp.250–1

10. 20 July. 'Islam and Progress', Part 4, 'The Command to Kill', *NA*, XIX, pp.272–5

11. 3 August. 'Islam and Progress', Part 5, 'The Brotherhood of All Believers', *NA*, XIX, pp.323–4

1917

1. January. 'The Prophet's Gratitude', *IRMI*, V, pp.35–9

2. February and March. 'Address on the Prophet's Birthday', *IRMI*, V, pp.53–9

3. 1 February. 'Oriental Encounters', Part 1, 'Rashid the Fair', *NA*, XX, pp.329–30

4. 22 February. 'Oriental Encounters', Part 2, 'A Mountain Garrison', *NA*, XX, pp.400–1

5. 8 March. 'Oriental Encounters', Part 3, 'The Rhinoceros Whip', *NA*, XX, pp.448–9

6. 22 March. 'Oriental Encounters', Part 4, 'The Courteous Judge', *NA*, XX, pp.498–9

7. 12 April. 'Oriental Encounters', Part 5, 'Bastirma', *NA*, XX, pp.567–8

8. 26 April. 'Oriental Encounters', Part 6, 'The Sack which Clanked', *NA*, XX, pp.613–14

9. 31 May. 'Oriental Encounters', Part 7, 'Police Work', *NA*, XXI, pp.115–16

10. August. 'Islam and Progress', Part 1, *IRMI*, V, pp.337–52

11. 3 August. 'Zionists in Palestine' (letter), *The Near East*, p.266

12. September. *Knights of Araby*, W. Collins and Co., London

13. September. 'Islam and Progress', Part 2, *IRMI*, V, pp.368–84

14. 11 October. 'Oriental Encounters', Part 8, 'The Knight Errant', *NA*, XXI, pp.510–11

15. 1 November. 'Oriental Encounters', Part 9, 'The Hanging Dog', *NA*, XXII, pp.14–15

16. 22 November. 'Oriental Encounters', Part 10, 'The Last Dragoman', *NA*, XXII, p.134

17. December. 'The Holy Prophet as Example', *IRMI*, V, pp.497–500

1918

1. January. 'Islam and Modernism', *IRMI*, VI, pp.5–11

2. 17 January. 'Oriental Encounters', Part 11, 'The Unwalled Garden', *NA*, XXII, pp.234–5

3. 28 February. 'Oriental Encounters', Part 12, 'Nawadir', *NA*, XXII, pp.358–9

4. 18 April. 'Oriental Encounters', Part 13, 'The Fanatic', *NA*, XXII, pp.488–9

5. 16 May. 'Oriental Encounters', Part 14, 'Tragedy', *NA*, XXIII, pp.42–4

6. June. *Oriental Encounters* (reprint of items 3–9, 14–16, 1917; 2–5, 7, 9, 11–12, 1918), W. Collins and Co., London; republished by A.A. Knopf, New York, 1926; and in Travellers' Library, Heinemann, London, 1929

7. 13 June. 'Oriental Encounters', Part 15, 'Pride and Fall', *NA*, XXIII, pp.106–7

8. July. 'The Kingdom of God', *IRMI*, VI, pp.279–90

9. 4 July. 'Oriental Encounters', Part 16, 'The He-Goat', *NA*, XXIII, pp.156–7

10. August. 'Concerning Religious Truths', *IRMI*, VI, pp.328–37

11. 8 August. 'Oriental Encounters', Part 17, 'The Atheist', *NA*, XXIII, pp.238–9

12. 22 August. 'Oriental Encounters', Part 18, 'Tigers', *NA*, XXIII, pp.272–3

13. December. 'The Prophet's Character', *IRMI*, VI, pp.429–31

1919

1. January. 'The Qur'an', *IRMI*, VII, pp.9–16

2. February. 'Worship', *IRMI*, VII, pp.57–61
3. March. 'Tolerance', *IRMI*, VII, pp.89–96
4. 20 March. 'The Perils of a Propaganda', *NA*, XXIV, pp.321–2
5. 27 March. 'A Survival of Barbarism', *NA*, XXIV, pp.337–8
6. April. 'The Imperial Government', *IRMI*, VII, pp.123–7
7. April. 'War and Religion', Part 1, *IRMI*, VII, pp.129–48
8. 3 April. 'The League of Nations and the British Empire', *NA*, XXIV, pp.353–4
9. 10 April. 'The Trouble in Egypt', *NA*, XXIV, pp.370–1
10. 17 April. 'A Page of History', *NA*, XXIV, pp.389–91
11. 17 April. 'A Correction' (letter), *NA*, XXIV, p.399
12. 24 April. 'The Act of God', *NA*, XXIV, pp.405–6
13. May. 'War and Religion', Part 2, *IRMI*, VII, pp.169–82
14. *War and Religion* (reprint of items 7 and 13), Basheer Muslim Library, Woking
15. 1 May. 'The Cause of Massacres', *NA*, XXV, pp.4–7
16. 1 May. 'The Literature of Turkey' (letter), *NA*, XXV, pp.14–15
17. 15 May. 'America and the Near East', *NA*, XXV, pp.36–7
18. 15 May. 'Asia and the Armenians' (letter), *NA*, XXV, pp.49–50
19. 29 May. 'Persia and England', *NA*, XXV, pp.76–7
20. 29 May. 'Asia and the Armenians' (letter), *NA*, XXV, p.91
21. June. 'Friday Sermons', Part 1, *IRMI*, VII, pp.225–40
22. 5 June. 'Our Own People', *NA*, XXV, pp.96–7
23. 12 June. 'Asia and the League of Nations', *NA*, XXV, pp.112–13
24. 19 June. 'For the Defence', *NA*, XXV, pp.128–9
25. 26 June. 'Routine or Policy', *NA*, XXV, pp.144–5
26. July–August. 'Friday Sermons', Part 2, *IRMI*, VII, pp.293–308
27. 3 July. 'The Case of Smyrna', *NA*, XXV, pp.160–1
28. 10 July. 'Between the Lines', *NA*, XXV, pp.176–7
29. 17 July. 'The Truth at Last', *NA*, XXV, pp.192–3
30. 24 July. 'The Lesson of Caucasus', *NA*, XXV, pp.209–10
31. 31 July. 'In Short', *NA*, XXV, pp.224–5
32. September. 'Friday Sermons', Part 3, *IRMI*, VII, pp.337–52
33. 11 September. 'Canards' (letter), *NA*, XXV, p.335
34. October. 'Friday Sermons', Part 4, *IRMI*, VII, pp.374–92
35. *Friday Sermons* (reprint of items 21, 26 and 32; and pp.378–92 of item 34), Basheer Muslim Library, Woking
36. December. *Sir Limpidus*, W. Collins and Co., London
37. December. 'The Position of Women in Islam', *IRMI*, VII, pp.439–45
38. December. 'In the Name of Allah', *IRMI*, VII, pp.453–4
39. December. 'What is Propaganda?', *IRMI*, VII, pp.460–3

1920

1. *Islam and Progress* (reprinted from Items 10 and 13, 1917), The Islamic Book Society, Azeez Manzil, Lahore
2. *Perangdalam tindjavan Islam dan Kristen* (translation of *War and Religion* into Indonesian), Al Ma'arif, Bandung (date uncertain)
3. January. 'Endurance and Sacrifice', *IRMI*, VIII, pp.13–18
4. February. 'A Sermon', *IRMI*, VIII, pp.43–7
5. 12 February. 'Candidus: An Old Translation' (letter), *NA*, XXVI, p.241
6. 25 March. 'Imperial Suicide' (letter), *NA*, XXVI, p.343
7. 'Sterne and Voltaire's *Candide*' (letter), *NA*, XXVI, p.391
8. 29 April. 'The Armenians' (letter), *NA*, XXVI, p.423

9. May. 'Syrian Independence', *Foreign Affairs*, I, pp.10–11
10. July. 'Massacres and the Turks: The Other Side', *Foreign Affairs*, Special Supplement, II, pp.xiv–xvi
11. October. 'The Religion of Abraham', *IRMI*, VIII, pp.370–5
12. November. 'Women's Rights in Islam', *IRMI*, VIII, pp.402–6
13. December. 'Fasting in Islam', *IRMI*, VIII, pp.454–61

1921

1. January. 'Conception of God in Islam', *IR*, IX, pp.11–21
2. March. *The Early Hours*, W. Collins and Co., London
3. 10 November. 'Present Situation in India', *Muslim Standard*, pp.4–5

1922

1. 19 January. 'England and Islam' (letter), *The Near East*, p.82
2. October. *As Others See Us*, W. Collins and Co., London

1923

1. November. 'The True Khilafat', *IR*, XI, pp.389–91

1924

1. September. 'The Quest', *Cornhill Magazine*, LVII, pp.366–82; reprinted in *The Best Short Stories of 1925: 1: English*, edited by Edward J. O'Brien and John Cournos, Jonathan Cape, London, pp.168–87
2. December. 'Islamic Tolerance in India', *IR*, XII, pp.431–4

1925

1. February. 'England and Arabia, The Typical Case of Bahreyn', *Foreign Affairs*, VI, pp.177–8
2. April–May. 'The Essential Fact of Revelation', *IR*, XIII, pp.140–5

1926

1. *Glanz, Liebe und Tod des Fischers Saïd* (translation of *Saïd the Fisherman* into German by Paul Fohr), Albert Langen, Munich
2. June. 'The Student and the Tower', *Cornhill Magazine*, LX, pp.682–93

1927

1. January. 'Muslim Education', *IC*, I, pp.100–8
2. January. 'Islamic Culture', *IC*, I, pp.151–63
3. April. 'Islamic Culture: Causes of its Rise and Decline', *IC*, I, pp.259–318
4. *The Cultural Side of Islam* (reprint of items 2 and 3), Committee of Madras Lectures on Islam, Madras; republished as *Islamic Culture*, Ferozsons, Lahore, 1958; republished as *The Cultural Side of Islam*, Kitab Bharan, New Delhi, 1981
5. July. '"Spiritualism" and Islam', *IC*, I, pp.488–97

A Pickthall Bibliography

1928

1. January. 'Shorter Notices' (review), *IC*, II, pp.158–61
2. April. 'The Kingdom of Bornu' (review), *IC*, II, pp.309–13
3. April. 'An Encyclopedia of Muslim Authors' (review), *IC*, II, pp.313–15
4. April. 'A Voyage in Algeria' (review), *IC*, II, pp.315–19
5. July. 'The Advance of Urdu', *IC*, II, pp.464–71
6. July. 'Russia and Turkey' (review), *IC*, II, pp.471–5
7. July. 'For Iran' (review), *IC*, II, pp.475–6

1929

1. April. 'Agrarian Reforms in Turkistan' (review), *IC*, III, pp.309–15
2. April. 'Syrian Folk-lore' (review), *IC*, III, pp.316–19
3. July. 'The Occult in Revealed Religion' (review), *IC*, III, pp.474–81
4. July. 'Indian Music' (review), *IC*, III, pp.482–6
5. October. 'Higgins' "Apology" ' (review), *IC*, III, pp.637–44
6. October. 'Mr Vakil at Ajanta' (review), *IC*, III, pp.644–6

1930

1. January. 'Mr Khuda Bukhsh's Sheaf of Gleanings from the German' (review), *IC*, IV, pp.161–8
2. January. 'The Legendary Aurangzeb' (review), *IC*, IV, pp.168–70
3. April. 'The Decorative Inscriptions of the Alhambra' (review), *IC*, IV, pp.329–30
4. July. 'The So-Called "Covenant of 'Umar" ' (review), *IC*, IV, pp.475–7
5. July. 'Mr Khuda Bukhsh's "Islamic Civilisation" ' Vol II (review), *IC*, IV, pp.477–9
6. July. 'New Cairo' (review), *IC*, IV, pp.480–5
7. October. 'The Bombay Mural Paintings' (review), *IC*, IV, pp.666–7
8. October. 'A Description of Islam in India' (review), *IC*, IV, pp.667–70
9. December. *The Meaning of the Glorious Koran*, A.A. Knopf, New York; republished in two volumes with Arabic text by Government Central Press, Hyderabad, 1938; republished as *The Glorious Koran* with Arabic text by Allen and Unwin, London, 1939; republished as *The Meaning of the Glorious Koran* by the New American Library, New York, 1953; republished with Arabic and Urdu translation by Fateh Muhammad Jallendhri, Kutubkhana Ishaat-ul-Islam, Delhi, 1970 (and reprinted by Taj Company, New Dehli, 1983); republished with Arabic text by Dar al Kitab, Beirut, 1971; republished with Arabic text, Tripoli, Libya, in about 1982; republished (English only) by Dar al Shoura, London, 1985. In 1980 a recording on 54 cassettes with certain alterations to the translation was issued under the patronage and at the expense of Sheikh Sultan bin Muhammad al Qasimi, Ruler of Sharjah, United Arab Emirates. The English text was read by Gai Eaton (Hasan Abdul Hakim)

1931

1. April. 'The Figure of the Prophet in Islamic Lore' (review), *IC*, V, pp.334–7
2. April. 'Four Hyderabad Writers of Good English Verse' (review), *IC*, V, pp.337–9
3. July. 'Arabs and Non-Arabs and the Question of Translating the Qur'an', *IC*, V, pp.422–33
4. July. 'Mahmud of Ghazna' (review), *IC*, V, pp.496–7
5. July. 'The Medley of Islam and Hinduism' (review), *IC*, V, pp.498–500

6. July. 'A Polemic of the Third Islamic Century' (review), *IC*, V, pp.500–2
7. July. 'The Glory of Aleppo' (review), *IC*, V, pp.503–4
8. July. 'An Aspect of Brahmacharya' (review), *IC*, V, pp.505–6
9. July. 'A Book of Folk-Tales' (review), *IC*, V, pp.506–8
10. July. 'A Hindu-Muslim Conversation in the Eleventh Century, AH' (review), *IC*, V, p.508
11. October. 'Sir Muhammad Iqbal's Lectures' (review), *IC*, V, pp. 677–83
12. October. 'A Concise World History of Islam' (review), *IC*, V, pp.683–4

1932

1. January. 'Westernising Persia' (review), *IC*, VI, pp.153–6
2. April. 'Old Hyderabad' (review), *IC*, VI, pp.319–25
3. April. 'New Turkey' (review), *IC*, VI, pp.325–7
4. July. 'The Damascus Chronicle of the Crusades' (review), *IC*, VI, pp.486–91
5. July. 'Sirdar Iqbal Ali Shah's Life of the Prophet' (review), *IC*, VI, pp.491–2
6. July. 'Education in India' (review), *IC*, VI, pp.492–3
7. July. 'The Tiger' (review), *IC*, VI, pp.497–8
8. July. 'Iraq-wa-Iran' (review), *IC*, VI, pp.498–500
9. October. 'Mr Vakil on Rock-Cut Temples' (review), *IC*, VI, pp.665–7
10. October. 'The New Education in Germany' (review), *IC*, VI, pp.667–9
11. October. 'Astrology as Religion' (review), *IC*, VI, pp.669–71

1933

1. January. 'Religion Universal and Eternal' (review), *IC*, VII, pp.160–7
2. January. 'The Quatrains of Hali' (review), *IC*, VII, pp.167–71
3. April. 'Professor Wensinck on Muslim Beliefs' (review), *IC*, VII, pp.335–8
4. April. 'Ghafiq's Book of Simples' (review), *IC*, VII, pp.338–41
5. April. 'The Art of the Mughals' (review), *IC*, VII, pp.341–3
6. April. 'Two Books on Sufism' (review), *IC*, VII, pp.347–51
7. July. 'A Pageant of Old Persia' (review), *IC*, VII, pp.506–10
8. July. 'The Faith of the Shi'a' (review), *IC*, VII, pp.511–14
9. July. 'Al-Andalus' (review), *IC*, VII, pp.514–16
10. October. 'Islamic Schools of Thought' (review), *IC*, VII, pp.682–5
11. October. 'Abu Nawas' (review), *IC*, VII, pp.686–9

1934

1. January. 'The Reformation of Islam' (review), *IC*, VIII, pp.150–3
2. January. 'The Qur'an and the Prophet' (review), *IC*, VIII, pp.156–63
3. January. 'An Arabic History of the Seljuqids' (review), *IC*, VIII, pp.163–5
4. January. 'Archaeology in Hyderabad' (review), *IC*, VIII, pp.165–8
5. January. 'The Toghluq-Nameh of Amir Khosru' (review), *IC*, VIII, pp.168–9
6. April. 'The Arabic Encyclopaedia of Islam' (review), *IC*, VIII, pp.322–4
7. April. 'The Assamese Chronicle' (review), *IC*, VIII, pp.324–8
8. April. 'The Ismaili Law of Wills' (review), *IC*, VIII, pp.328–9
9. April. 'Recent Urdu Publications' (review), *IC*, VIII, pp.329–37
10. July. 'The Isma'ili Classics' (review), *IC*, VIII, pp.494–7
11. July. 'Pictorial Representations of the Ka'bah' (review), *IC*, VIII, pp.504–6
12. July. 'The Claims of Islam' (review), *IC*, VIII, pp.506–7
13. October. 'The Need of the Sunnah' (review), *IC*, VIII, pp.665–8

14. October. 'Al-Andalus Vol II Part I' (review), *IC*, VIII, pp.668–70
15. October. 'An English Lady's Pilgrimage' (review), *IC*, VIII, pp.674–9
16. October. 'The Phonetics of Eastern Turkish' (review), *IC*, VIII, pp.679–81

1935

1. January. 'Kitabu'l-Awraq' (review), *IC*, IX, pp.172–4
2. January. '"The Prophet of the Desert"' (review), *IC*, IX, pp.174–6
3. January. 'Law and Justice in Modern India' (review), *IC*, IX, pp.176–9
4. January. 'The Pedigree of the Fatimids' (review), *IC*, IX, 179–81
5. January. 'The Arab Question' (review), *IC*, IX, pp.182–3
6. January. 'Kabul' (review), *IC*, IX, pp.183–4
7. January. 'Mr Probsthain's Oriental Catalogue' (review), *IC*, IX, pp.184–5
8. April. 'The Early Years of Islam' (review), *IC*, IX, pp.368–70
9. April. 'Islam and Civilisation' (review), *IC*, IX, p.370
10. April. 'Mubtala' (review), *IC*, IX, p.371
11. April. 'A Turkish Woman's Love Story' (review), *IC*, IX, pp.372–4
12. July. 'Mr Yusuf Ali's Translation of the Qur'an' (review), *IC*, IX, p.519–21
13. July. 'An Old Turk Reformer' (review), *IC*, IX, pp.527–9
14. July. 'Arabic and Russian Poetry' (review), *IC*, IX, pp.529–31
15. October. 'The End of a Legend' (review), *IC*. IX, pp.665–7
16. October. 'Artificial Nation-Building' (review), *IC*, IX, pp.667–70
17. October. 'The Successors of Sher Shah' (review), *IC*, IX, pp.670–1
18. October. 'The "Esoteric" Doctrine' (review), *IC*, IX, pp.671–3
19. October. 'A Notable Arabic Publication' (review), *IC*, IX, pp.673–4
20. October. 'A Pahlavi-Persian Grammar' (review), *IC*, IX, pp.674–5

1936

1. January. 'Kitabu'l-Awraq Vol II' (review), *IC*, X, pp.153–8
2. January. 'The Doctrine of the Sufis' (review), *IC*, X, pp.148–62
3. January. 'Hyderabad Reforms' (review), *IC*, X, pp.162–3
4. January. 'The Princes of Arcot' (review), *IC*, X, pp.163–5
5. April. 'Pictorial Hyderabad' (review), *IC*, X, pp.335–6
6. April. 'The Muslims in the Modern World', *Journal of the Central Asian Society*, XXII, pp.221–35 and 294
7. April. 'Hyderabad the Heart of India', *Geographical Magazine*, no. 6, pp.400–20
8. July. 'The Turkish Experiment' (review), *IC*, X, pp.486–92
9. July. 'A Descriptive Catalogue of the Arabic, Persian and Urdu Manuscripts in the Library of the University of Bombay' (review), *IC*, X, pp.498–9
10. July. 'Al-Qalqashandi on India' (review), *IC*, X, pp.503–4
11. October. 'The Perfect Policy' (review), *IC*, X, pp.659–62
12. October. 'Alamgir the Great' (review), *IC*, X, pp.662–6
13. October. 'The Story of India' (review), *IC*, X, pp.666–8

1937

1. January. 'The Two Voices' (review), *IC*, XI, pp.150–4
2. July. 'Letters from Turkey', *IC*, XI, pp.419–32

1948

1. *Saïd Il Pescatore* (translation of *Saïd the Fisherman* into Italian by O. Nemi), Longanesi, Milan

1958

1. *Kur'âni Kerim ve Hazreti Muhammad* (translation of the introduction of *The Meaning of the Glorious Koran* into Turkish by Şinasi Siber), in the series of the Religious Affairs Directorate, printed by Ayyildiz Matbaasi, Ankara
2. *Kur'âni Kerimin Manalari* (translation of part of *The Meaning of the Glorious Koran* into Turkish by M. Şevki Alay and Ali Kâtiboğlu), Hadise Yayinevi, Istanbul

1964

1. *Al Corão* (translation of *The Meaning of the Glorious Koran* into Portuguese), Bento de Castro, Lourenço Marques

INDEX

Index

Index